SECRET VOICES

FROM

THE FOREST

Thoughts and Dreams of North American Trees

VOLUME ONE: THE WEST

Text and
Illustrations by

Laura J. Merrill

Myth and Magic
Taos, NM

Claire —
you've been a
good friend.
Love,
Laura

Published by: Myth & Magic
               PO Box 612
               Taos, NM 87571
               laurajmerrilltreetalker.com

ISBN-13 978-0-9848299-0-3

Library of Congress Control Number: 2011960508

All poems by permission, © Brian R. Mitchell
All photographs © Laura J. Merrill
Artwork photographed by Andrew Neighbour
Cover/interior design by Mary Neighbour and Laura J. Merrill
Edited by Jénnet Grover

Printed in China

First Edition

10 09 08 07 06 05 04 03 02 01

CONTENTS

CHAPTER TWO

Southern Pacific Coast: Mediterranean Chaparral and Riparian Woodlands

California Sycamore

Mexican Elder

California Bay Laurel

PART TWO: THE INTERMOUNTAIN WEST

CHAPTER THREE

The Pacific Coast Ranges and The Great Basin

CHAPTER FOUR

The Rocky Mountains: Columbia, Colorado, and
Wasatch Temperate Coniferous Forests

< v >

< Thoughts and Dreams of North American Trees >

< **vi** >

< Secret Voices from the Forest >

FOREWORD

There are books that come into your life stay for a while and then disappear, maybe on loan, a place of mystery from which few books ever return. Sometimes they get left behind on trains, planes and in hotel bedrooms. They are the "Hobos" of the book world and were never meant to stay with you. Others lie around snoozing on dusty shelves only waking when you suddenly remember a favorite chapter. There are books that teach, books that hold history between their pages and books that make you laugh. A few, a very few, become close friends that stay with you and maybe . . . when you are old, are passed on to special people. This is such a book.

I love Trees, a garden is nice, beautiful, either wild or tamed but garden flowers are basically the Showgirls of the plant world. Wild Flowers are the chorus, bright, cheerful a little gaudy sometimes, but always ready to greet you. But Trees! Trees are my love. They are the wise ones of the Plant world, the history keepers, the elders. Tolkien knew this and wrote of them as The Ents.

< vii >

I met the author at a workshop and my attention was caught by the myriad shades of greens that flowed around her like mist. She smelt of Trees, that sharp green odor that reminds you of freshly cut lawns and wide meadows filled waist high with wild flowers and grass. She talked about a book she was writing and shyly asked if I would write a foreword. She showed me pictures and described her work among the Plant life of this planet and I knew it would be something worth waiting for. Now it is here.

Every page is a delight, an adventure, an explanation of something not always rare, but seen and described with a depth that borders on the miraculous. The Trees are there, but so are the leaves, the fruit, their inner meanings and powers. There are small creatures, birds and insects that use them for homes, food, watch towers, and playgrounds. This is not just a book about Trees, it is a book about the beings with whom we share this planet. Trees are very much like people. People that don't walk about but who make their home in one place and have a deep community spirit with the other life forms that share that space with them. This is not just a book of, or for information, it is a book about the life-forms that share the planet with us, feel, breathe, grow, give birth, fall ill, get old, and die. Just like us.

Just look around you and see how much Trees have given us. Houses, furniture, toys, fruit, paper, seeds, nuts, shelter, shade and sweetened rejuvenated air. We give little in return. We burn them, cut them down, poison them, and damage them, and not only them but the smaller lives that depend on them. The author has set before us a panoramic viewpoint of the world about us.

< Thoughts and Dreams of North American Trees >

The illustrations alone are worth the price, the knowledge and love of the subject and the painstaking care with which she shares with us her soul's deep appreciation of the "Green World" make this something to treasure. Give this book to someone you love deeply, give it to someone who never has time to sit under a tree and dream. Give it to someone who loves their garden, but has never really got to know it at the spiritual level. Give it to young people so they can get to know the wonder of Trees and their kindred, give to busy people who may then take the time to discover what they have missed, give to elderly people who maybe cannot get out to see the world they once knew.

When I began to read I knew only how to recognise an Oak, a Holly, a Copper Beech, and maybe a Chestnut, but now I can walk into a wood and name so many more. I have learned about the tiny life forms that surround us, most of the time unseen and un-noticed. I have discovered a world that is so much more than simply "trees."

After nearly fifty years of reading, learning, and teaching about the "Tree of Life" I have discovered the original of that idea and feel blessed by that discovery.

Dolores Ashcroft-Nowicki
Director of Studies, SOL
Jersey, United Kingdom
August 2011

PREFACE

It may surprise some to find that trees have not held any unusual significance for me until recently. Like many others before me, I have always found them beautiful, or peaceful—just *there*, in a neighborly, reliable sort of way.

My cousin Ken introduced me to arboreal study when I was twelve, on my visit to his family in Huntington, West Virginia. There were extensive woods near their house, and he spent a couple of days showing me a rather impressive variety of trees, whose leaves we collected and placed in a scrapbook. It might have been fair to call *him* a Tree Lover, but no one would have said that about me.

So, forty-five years later, when I was "assigned" the writing of this book, it seemed to come out of nowhere.

Well, not *quite* out of nowhere.

Dolores Ashcroft-Nowicki travels to North America, generally once a year, giving lectures about a variety of esoteric subjects, and in September of 2006, I was an attendee at her three-day seminar about Celtic Tree Magic. As we were nearing the end of the workshop, I enquired whether the topic had ever been updated or extended to cover trees of North America, as we have species here that do not exist in the British Isles. "No," she said, "but *you* could do it, and you could write a book!"

So here we are.

I describe this interchange as an "assignment," not because Dolores expected *me*, particularly, to take on this project, but because, as she spoke, I had the intense impression that she was acting as conduit for some outside force. What that force was, I could not say. It might have been as simple as my own unconscious, but I chose to believe it was from a "group mind" type of energy—from *Trees* as a whole.

At any rate, I took it seriously.

During the next year, I considered how to proceed. Should this only be about trees exclusive to North America? Should it cover trees that were already part of the Celtic Tree Alphabet? What kind of information needed to be included? Eventually, since writing had never been my forte, I decided to start drawing—something with which I *did* have experience. It seemed logical to begin with a picture of a Sagebrush plant, since my home is in the middle of a sea of Sagebrush.

That seemed to get the energy moving, as the next obvious move was to take a long drive around the West, to visit the famous trees of several National Parks. It also seemed like the perfect opportunity to visit with old friends along the way—in New Mexico, California, Utah and British Columbia, Canada. Each of them, oddly enough, had little "messages" for me, such as, "Do this now, because the idea is in the air, and if you don't do it, someone else will."

As the journey progressed, I met some of my future subjects–the saguaro cactus, the Joshua tree, the coastal redwood and the giant sequoia. The structure of the book began to suggest itself, and I returned home to begin my commission.

Without describing, blow-by-blow, the ongoing occurrence of small "inspirations," I will say that each step, no matter how small, has "presented" itself to me, sometimes through advice from friends, but more often as what seemed the logical thing to do next. This has been a lesson in following the voice of one's unconscious, whomever is its channel.

The trees in this volume, *The West*, have been chosen to be representatives of the western region of North America. It has been divided into four chapters: "Northern Pacific Coast—Temperate Rainforest," "Southern Pacific Coast—Mediterranean Chaparral and Riparian Woodlands," "The Coast Ranges and Great Basin," which includes the Cascades and Sierra Nevada Mountain Ranges and the arid plateaus and drainage basins west of the Continental Divide, and, finally, "The Rockies." Each area is briefly described to set a "stage" for the three trees selected to exemplify it.

An *individual* tree's segment begins with its portrait and a short piece called "Reflections," which is intended to represent the tree's thoughts, as I interpret them through my meditations. This is followed by a descriptive account of the tree and interesting related facts. Finally, there is a listing of the tree's Companions, which are other species found within the same ecosystem, a portrait page designed specifically for the Companions, and a few entertaining facts about some of them. The Companions' portrait page contains a verse, written as though the tree itself were speaking. I conclude each chapter with some thoughts of my own.

This book, the first of four, is subtitled *The West*. The second volume, as it will concern itself with the trees of the plains and the midwest, will be subtitled *Midcontinent*; the third, with the trees of *The East*; and the fourth, with those of the *Tropics and Deserts*. Each of these volumes will be structured identically, so the number of trees ultimately represented will be forty-eight.

Selecting the Trees

When speaking to friends who live at a distance, I find they sometimes express surprise or disapproval of a particular choice of a tree species to represent their home region. Patriotism applies to just about anything, it seems, so I will attempt to explain the methods by which the trees included in a particular area have been chosen.

The first criterion is that each species must be indigenous to part of the North American continent, not necessarily exclusively, although several are. To my Mexican and Canadian neighbors, I admit that there is a predominance of trees that occurs primarily in the United States, but I have endeavored to ignore imaginary borders as much as possible.

The second criterion is that each of my choices is *considered* to be a tree, at least by *some* authority. The standards are that the subject must be at least thirteen feet high, even if only

< x >

< Secret Voices from the Forest >

in ideal conditions, and it must have a woody stem. That allows for several species, which, under less than ideal circumstances, would be considered shrubs, like mountain mahogany and Gambel oak.

My third criterion is variety. Since the ultimate number of trees included will be limited, I have had to be quite selective from the outset. Regretfully, there will be many unique, fascinating species that will be passed over. Having said that, it will be noted that two of the existing three species of redwood are represented—indeed, how could I not include both coastal redwood and the giant sequoia? My justification is that they are: a) very different from each other; b) completely unique in the world (although millions of years ago that was not the case, as both existed in Europe and Asia); and c) both thoroughly spectacular, a fact which no one would dispute.

To those in California who lament the exclusion of the coastal and valley live oaks, my intent is to use the live oak of the Gulf Coast region. As that particular species is almost universally identified with the South, it seems a more fitting representative of that region. In order to include as many different species as possible, a lot of shuffling and stretching has occurred.

Sometimes a species that occurs less often than another very similar one in its family was selected so that there would be space for something else later. Case in point: western serviceberry, which occurs rather sparsely compared to its Eastern cousins.

After variety, things get a little more haphazard. The area west of the Rocky Mountains has a predominance of, and a much greater variety of softwoods, or conifers, while east of the Missouri River, hardwoods, or deciduous tree species, are greater in number and diversity. In the Midwest and Great Plains, the choices are fewer in number. This fact was helpful, by process of elimination, in the selection of trees for the eastern regions.

< xi >

For instance, there are so many different species of conifers—sixty-five species in the Pine Family alone, which includes pine, spruce and fir—that only a very notable few could be included. On the other hand, I did not want the content of *The West* to be exclusively conifers and *The East* exclusively deciduous, so that meant that even fewer pines would make the final cut.

I found ways of including a further few individuals: first, by selecting one or two additional trees to be pictured as one of the Companions, second, by placing an unidentified tree in a painting as a member of "the neighborhood," and third, by grouping several trees together in a collective system, such as the "old growth forest."

The Companions

I decided early in its development that this project should be more than a collection of artwork and snippets about trees. It should also touch upon the larger concept of *ecosystems*, in which plants and animals are in symbiotic relationship with the land and each other.

The selected plants and animals are referred to as *The Companions*, and have a separate page upon which they are portrayed, as a group. Their portraits, consisting of drawings of

< Thoughts and Dreams of North American Trees >

nine animals and nine plants that occur within the tree's environment, form a "frame" for the poem from the tree with which they are associated. The Companions are listed, in clockwise order, on the opposite page.

I picked two mammals, two birds, two reptiles and/or amphibians, two insects and/or spiders and/or crustaceans and made one purely random choice for each tree.

The plants included two trees and/or shrubs, usually one fungus, sometimes a species of grass, and the rest, flowering plants of one kind or another.

They are not the only fauna and flora in that environment, nor even necessarily the most important, nor do they only, or even primarily, occur in that environment. Mainly, the goal was to pick species that were colorful and interesting.

All were chosen using the excellent field guides published by the Audubon Society, The National Geographic Society, The National Wildlife Federation, and the Roger Tory Peterson Institute.

It was a pleasure and an education to learn about and illustrate such a large variety of the Earth's inhabitants. (Who knew that beetles make up one-fourth of all animal species on earth?)

It has also been delightful to see some of the birds I included as Companions actually appear at the birdfeeder. Having had the opportunity to study them, I now know what they are called. However, it seems unlikely that they have the slightest concern about what I, or others, have elected to name them.

Laura J. Merrill
July 2011

< xii >

< Secret Voices from the Forest >

INTRODUCTION

The Celts of Northern Europe and the British Isles long ago developed a cryptic alphabet, called the *Ogham*, in which the letters represented tree names. Some speculate that it was a secret code, known only to the Druids, by which they passed on their knowledge of magic, while others claim it was used in a more common manner, primarily to mark graves and designate property borders. Many believe that the attributes of the trees were also meant to be a part of the language, although little record remains of the authors' original intent.

Whatever the truth, this system has inspired academic controversy, several books on the subject and, what is more important, a focus-point for many who have discovered a renewed sense of reverence for the Earth and its potentially unique capacity to harbor an infinite array of life forms.

At present, the trees in this alphabetic system, and the mystical significance they are each accorded, are seen as metaphors for steps on the path of one's spiritual journey through life.

However, the Ogham is rooted many hundreds of years in the past, in ancient knowledge relevant to a long-forgotten world. When the meanings of these symbols were fresh in the minds of the Celtic Bards, the wild forest was close at hand and seemingly impenetrable — a place of shadowy mysteries and frightening spirits. Contact with people who lived somewhere on its nether borders involved a long, arduous, and often dangerous passage.

Today, most of us never think about dark forests. Our species has spread over the globe, establishing enormous, sprawling metropolises where the once-threatening animals and plants have been contained, their only permitted habitats zoos, parks, botanic gardens and manicured yards. The perils we formerly associated with existence — being eaten by a tiger or bitten by a snake — have been replaced by the dangers of city dwelling — traffic, pollution and crime. Travel is now an activity we engage in for business or relaxation. When we wish, we can journey thousands of miles in a single day, or communicate with someone on the opposite side of the planet in a nanosecond.

Our current cities and way of life would be unrecognizable to the people that created the alphabet of the Ogham. We have become, without a doubt, the dominant species, and the only real threats facing us are of our own making.

Throughout the development of civilization, in our efforts to protect ourselves, we have often regarded Nature as something we must war against. But it seems that the more we have managed to insulate ourselves from perceived dangers, the more we have become removed from our own nature, arriving at the conclusion that we have only a peripheral relationship to the "products" derived from once-living creatures, now wrapped in sanitary plastic at the market.

Joseph Campbell spoke often about how indigenous cultures, specifically the American Indian tribes, regarded all things in creation — the rivers and mountains, the trees and animals — as sacred. Not "it," but "thou." Everything derived from them was also sacred, a gift from the Great Spirit.

Sadly, it seems we have, as a global community, arrived at a functional reality very far from those early beliefs. There is no way to turn back the clock, nor should we try. The ongoing scientific discovery of the workings and makeup of the physical universe can be incorporated in our developing regard for the planet. The more we learn about the minute, intricate ways in which environmental systems and life forms tightly intertwine, the more genuine awe and respect for the planet will be accorded.

Green spaces in cities, parks and gardens offer welcome relief from the pace of urban living, and rooftop and community vegetable plots allow for hands-on interaction with growing things. It is possible to learn a great deal about nature, as well as about oneself, by spending time alone with the trees of an arboretum or a National Park.

Alone, without distraction from others, we can experience nature as a living presence with which we can interact, rather than only observing it on a television screen. We can learn to be sensitive to the elements of our surroundings, as well as to have an awareness of what could be called the "atmospheres" created by a combination of factors: the songs and chatter of birds and squirrels, the rustle of leaves and branches on a windy day, the stillness amongst the trees in which you can sense that you are seen by the beings that encircle you, but are not judged.

Of course, people create atmospheres, but it is not difficult to feel the difference between the atmosphere of an office environment and that of Sequoia National Park.

It is also not difficult to sense the difference between the atmospheres of the National Parks of Sequoia and Acadia, Banff and the Yucatan, or the Everglades and Saguaro.

The emanations of a specific species of tree are different as well. They themselves are individual in nature, as well as having sometimes quite unique relationships with plants and animals of their immediate surroundings.

< xiv >

The Brazil Nut Tree in the Amazon Rainforest of South America needs a visit from a specific bee in order to be pollinated. It has recently been ascertained that by slashing and burning the forest to create cropland, we have divided the forest into small, disconnected "islands," and as a result, the trees are ceasing to produce nuts.

Nature abounds with examples of these symbiotic relationships between plants and animals in a specific area — they are part of an *ecosystem*, which is defined as a system formed by the interaction of a community of organisms with its environment, and includes geological factors and weather conditions.

While many plants and animals have adapted themselves to a variety of systems, there are those who live exclusively in one area or in relation to one plant or animal. Of course, these organisms are in the greatest danger of extinction when conditions go through a drastic alteration.

Archaeological evidence has shown us that the Earth has undergone numerous mass extinctions, climactic upheavals, and geothermal and geological events that have dramatically changed the face of the planet. We fear these occurrences, as they present challenges that may threaten the continuation of life itself; however, the very instability of Earth's interacting processes is what creates this many-faceted Paradise.

We humans are also an element of this huge bio-system, and if we are to continue into the future with any quality of life, we should view this time as the infancy of an era in which we have the chance to recognize our true function in the experiment of Life on Planet Earth. We are not gods, angels, demons, or even stewards, but a form of life that has acquired awareness — not only of *self*, but of others, as well. This is our gift and our task, as it carries great responsibility.

It has been said that humans are "life experiencing itself" through this form. It follows

< Secret Voices from the Forest >

then, that all life forms, plant and animal, are a part of the same process—life experiencing itself, no less valid or valuable than we humans.

Although it differs greatly from us in form, in actuality, the plant world has preceded us as the great explorer-race, venturing into virtually every part of the globe, in an astounding variety of shapes and forms. Surely these ancient journeyers have learned much about this biosphere, and have a great deal they can tell us about the world and themselves—more than what our scientists can discover of their physical attributes and functions.

I believe that the trees themselves can aid us in our pursuit of awareness of other life forms. We can benefit from their plant-knowledge, first, because their history on this planet predates ours by such a degree, and second, simply *because* their form is so different. But how is that possible?

We know that our thoughts and feelings are the same as another person's because we share the expression of them. We have language. Even then, unless the effort is made by each party to understand the language of the other, communication is not possible.

In the many incarnations of *Star Trek*, members of the crew would often meet other species of intelligent beings that were so unlike themselves as to be unrecognizable as sentient. Fortunately, they were in possession of a wonderful Universal Translator that could be switched on, magically rendering all squeaks, grunts, whistles and clicks comprehensible.

Since the great Gnome project, researchers have discovered that plants' DNA is often several times more complicated than humans. Isn't it feasible that plants interface with each other via communication systems that are structured *entirely differently* from those of humans? These systems could be infinitely more efficient than ours. After all, plants are the vastly more ancient inhabitants of our planet, by many millions of years—so might we, as new kids on the block, be able to learn from their experience?

Are trees sentient? As yet, there is no body of scientific knowledge proving, without any doubt, that this is the case. I believe that just as we are still discovering the fascinating workings of DNA, we will eventually discover, at the core of *all* life is the same driving power and consciousness. This consciousness may take a multiplicity of forms, but on some level, the communicating element is the same.

We don't have a Universal Translator—at least not yet—but we can develop awareness of our surroundings, and extend that awareness out further from the people in our lives, to the greater world of plants and animals.

The mystical relationship the Celts had so long ago with the trees of Northern Europe and the British Isles is one that can give us a jumping-off point for a new relationship with the trees of here and now, with nature in general, and thereby help us define our role in a sustainable future. This new relationship, while still concerned with the workings of the human mind and spirit, would focus on the greater needs of the planet.

Why appear in all these forms? I cannot answer that, but I would guess it is something along the lines of a spiritual version of "Be All That You Can Be." So, in our search for wisdom, we should consult with other forms of life, and seek their unique knowledge.

As with the ancient Tree Ogham, some of this wisdom will be relayed in metaphor, but some truths are apparently universal to all forms of life. They still can tell us about ourselves, but in relation to the greater world around us, of which they, too, are a part.

CHAPTER ONE

NORTHERN PACIFIC COAST
TEMPERATE RAINFOREST

from the moss-darkened forest floor
a dragonfly's
jeweled signaling

NORTHERN PACIFIC COAST:
TEMPERATE RAINFOREST

Temperate rainforests are found along coasts, between the tropics and the poles, both north and south of the equator. The world's largest are on the Pacific coasts of North America, from northern California through southern Alaska.

The climate is more extreme than that of a tropical rainforest. In summer, temperatures can rise to nearly 80°, and in winter, drop to nearly freezing, so evergreen broadleaf trees are replaced by evergreen coniferous species, which are better adapted to shed snow and to photosynthesize in cold temperatures. Decomposition of forest litter happens more slowly, due to the acidity of conifer needles, as well as the colder temperatures. A large tree that falls can take hundreds of years to decompose—almost as long as it did to reach its great size.

With the generally colder climate, and its dominance of coniferous tree species, comes a reduction in species of plants and animals, in comparison to a tropical rainforest. An acre of tropical rainforest can hold literally hundreds of tree species, whereas the same sized area of temperate rainforest may contain less than a dozen. The dominant tree species in the Pacific rainforests are the Sitka spruce, western hemlock, western redcedar, and Douglas fir, along with the coastal redwood, and vary in combination, depending on location.

The temperate rainforests of North America are relatively small in collective area, and are made up of a number of *microclimates*. These microclimates vary according to the type and density of the forest canopy, which influences the amount of sunlight reaching the forest floor, the ambient air temperature, and wind velocity within the forest.

As with the tropical rainforest, the main factor affecting the environment is water. Rainfall can be as much as 165 inches per year, as it is in the Hoh rainforest, on the Olympic Peninsula in Washington State. Winters have the most precipitation, and although the summers can produce drought, the coastal fog usually compensates for any deficit of moisture.

The proximity of the Pacific Ocean is a major factor in the climate, moderating the temperatures and amount of rainfall. The average annual temperatures range between 38° and 56° Fahrenheit. The warmest regions are along the Pacific coast, with its humid, marine conditions, while above the tree line, arctic conditions may occur.

These forests are among the most productive in North America and contain some of the world's largest and long-lived trees. Many trees reach well over 300 feet in height. The northern Pacific coast forests house the most massive ecosystem on the planet. Including living and decaying trees, mosses, shrubs, and soil, they contain about 500 tons of biomass per acre, which is four times greater than any comparable area of tropical rainforest.

A temperate rainforest grows in four main layers, with different trees, flowers, and other plants in each layer. The top layer is called the *emergent* layer, where the tallest trees receive the most sunlight. The second layer is the *canopy*, which consists of tall trees growing close together, so that their tops form a continuous cover. The third layer is the *understory*, made up of smaller trees, bushes, and plants, such as ferns, which primarily receive indirect sunlight. The fourth layer is the *forest floor*, where there are mosses, algae, lichens, and other shade-loving plants.

The ground is littered with dead needles, leaves, twigs, and fallen trees. This slowly decomposing carpet of dead matter provides food and shelter for the animals and insects inhabiting the forest floor, and nourishment that is returned to the trees through their symbiotic relationships with fungi and soil bacteria.

Epiphytes are a common feature of all rainforests. An epiphyte is a plant that lives on the surface of another plant, but is non-parasitic, and derives its moisture and nutrients from the air and rain, and sometimes from debris accumulating around it. Examples of epiphytes occurring in the northwestern temperate rainforests are liverworts, lichens, algae, and club mosses, which are a very primitive type of plant. They often grow on trees to take advantage of sunlight in the canopy. In many areas of the rainforest, dense growths of mosses cover the trees, and ferns are a part of the lush under-story.

About 200 million years ago, the landscape of the planet was dominated by conifers, which not only constituted the majority of all trees existing at that time, but also had greater diversity of species than other plants of the era. Flowering plants, emerging around sixty-five million years ago, created the food supply for a seed only after it was fertilized. Primitive conifers invested their energy in the basic food supply for *every* seed. This reproductive difference allowed flowering plants to quickly displace the conifers, most of which became extinct. Those that survived had to adapt to harsh conditions.

‹ 3 ›

Now, the Pacific temperate rainforest is the only region on Earth of size and significance where the conifers flourish as they did before the emergence of flowering plants. This is due to the region's unique climatic conditions, which were created following the last ice age, about 20,000 years ago.

≼ COASTAL REDWOOD ≽

REFLECTIONS on FANTASY

What Redwood Can Tell You About Itself

The clouds and mist pressing in from the ocean have inspired me to want to stretch up as high as I am able. These translucent, amorphous particles are tiny beings that can journey anywhere. They soar into the sky, and delve far below the surface of the seas, so they can tell all, to those who will listen.

Being at the top is only an illusion. There is always something higher, something bigger. When I finally reach a place above all the others, I can see that I am still below, and contained, by the heavens. But I have also learned, through striving to go higher and higher, that the earth *beneath* me is the source of my power.

My kind knows of an ancient, secret realm in the lofty mountains of memory. It can never be reached, never be known or comprehended by those whose growth is finite. If the goal is to discover this realm, it will be necessary to abandon safety and security, and reach for the stars.

We understand why the deer hide, and we provide a place for them to disappear. In the kingdom of the Spirit, the deer are themselves creatures composed of mist—an idea of fleet-footedness becoming manifest. But the idea is very fragile, and slips in and out of the world of the dense physical, like sunlight on the forest floor.

Sunlight itself is animate. If something exists, it is filled with life and energy, even if that life is in transition. I have been a ray of sunlight here, in this forest. It was such a joyful experience that I decided to stay and become *Tree*. From this vantage point, I can see that the complexion of the sky changes as you rise up into it, and the bright displays of sunrises and sunsets become sharper and more vibrant.

Redwood's Place in the World

Redwood is an expression of the motivating and inspiring power of *Fantasy*. There is nothing unreal about Fantasy—it gives us the ambition to move and grow, to go outside of static reality where we can *become* our dreams. Fantasy is also a way of describing the space *between* everything, which we must move through to reach our desired destination. The universe behaves in this fashion as well, so Redwood demonstrates that you may think of the manifesting force of the universe as Fantasy.

The Redwood is unique in its curiosity about what is "out there;" it sees everything—the blackness of space, star systems exploding in and out of existence, or the nightly passage of the moon as movement in the flow of the life-blood of the universe. It interprets what it witnesses to indicate that we are a part of this movement as well, not unlike an organ in the body.

We are still discovering the functions of the organs of our *own* bodies; what do you suppose the function of our Solar System is within the larger body of the Universe? By giving your imagination permission to extend beyond its immediate circumstances, you may encounter the Future—within the remembrance of what has always been—and the Past, where all Life has its origins.

So much is possible within the Infinite; curiosity is inescapable. Redwood makes us wonder if time really exists, or if death may not be the position at which we start over when our present form has reached its limit. Perhaps death gives us the opportunity to try something different and extraordinary, to employ new genetic responses to changing conditions. Desire takes many forms, but it is always moving away from a static point. One thing grows out of another, so Desire must be the essence of life.

Redwood's Message for Us

The noise of conflict is more affecting than you know; it is invasive, and creates separation. Although this may be what the future holds, it would be pleasant to experience the peace that comes from looking up and out, observing, and even *seeing*.

Understanding we trees' comprehension of fantasy could help you on your race to the top. You should realize that you are pulling everything and everyone along with you, and this needs to be reflected in your attitude. Let it become not a race, but a form of transportation in which you are the "beast of burden" for the Planet as it attempts to elevate its consciousness.

You are capable of constructing tangible reality out of thin air. You bring into manifestation things that have never before existed, so the challenge is to use fantasy as a creative force, rather than a means of escape. Your function is to clear the way for the future, whatever it may be.

The force of the Unconscious is strong. When you teach yourself to become aware of the motivating purposes behind your own actions, two things will happen: first, you will cease to live in mental conflict, and second, you will be able to hear the voice of the Earth, and align yourself to her collective mind. It is not wise to "compete against" the rest of life—if you exclude yourself, you will ultimately be excluded.

Humans are an agent of change, and cannot avoid the consequences of being so. The threat of cataclysm might seem inevitable, but many factors, many elements in nature, defy prediction (although you love to try), and they will determine the ultimate outcome.

The future is a mystery that has yet to unfold. Take a long break from your everyday concerns, and then spend time looking at the darkness of the nighttime sky—it will give you *real* perspective.

CHRONICLES

The Coastal Redwood first appeared in the Mesozoic era, 250 to 65 million years ago. In fact, at that time there were over 150 species of Redwood worldwide. Today, only three members of this branch of the Cypress family remain: the coastal redwood and the giant sequoia, both in North America, and the dawn redwood, which is native to China.

These and other Conifers were the dominant plant life, along with gigantic ferns and mosses. Also appearing during this time were the flying reptiles, birds, and the land-based reptiles that would eventually develop into the dinosaurs of the Jurassic and Cretaceous periods that have become so familiar to us today.

All forms of life on this planet have mutually advantageous associations with the world of microscopic organisms. When the redwoods were emerging as a species, they formed associations with a particular type of fungi that penetrated the root tips of the trees, transferring nutrients, particularly phosphorus, from the soil. This particular fungus functioned well in warm, wet environments.

Beginning around twenty million years ago, the area that the redwoods occupied began to be gradually reduced, as the climate became colder and the soil dryer. The pines, whose fungal associates are of a type that do not penetrate root tissues as deeply, were better able to survive the climactic

< 7 >

< Northern Pacific Coast : Temperate Rain Forest : Coastal Redwood >

changes. They helped push out the redwoods, and eventually assumed the predominance they now have amongst conifer species.

Coastal redwoods now occupy a narrow strip of land from southern Oregon to central California, which is about 470 miles in length, but extends less than fifty miles inland–only as far as the coastal climate has its influence.

Fog is vital for the survival of these trees, protecting them from summer drought. A tree can acquire nearly 600 gallons of moisture daily from fog—almost 40% of its water requirements in summer. Redwoods also need abundant winter rain, as well as a range of temperatures that will not go far below freezing or above 100°. When conditions are ideal, a coastal redwood can grow 2-3 feet in height annually, but when the trees are stressed from lack of moisture and sunlight, they may grow as little as one inch per year.

Redwood trees flower during the wet, rainy months of December and January, and have both male and female flowers on the same plant. The flowers produce cones about an inch long, with tiny seeds, about the same size as those of a tomato. While each tree can produce 100,000 seeds annually, the germination rate is minimal.

Most redwoods grow more successfully from sprouts, which spontaneously emerge within the circumference of the tree trunk. Within a short period after sprouting, each sprout will develop its own root system, with the dominant sprouts forming a ring of trees around the parent root crown or stump. Sprouts can grow up to eight feet in a single growing season. When the parent tree dies, a new generation of trees arises, becoming sixty-five feet tall in twenty years. This ring of trees is called a "fairy ring."

The coastal redwood is a very long-lived tree, some individuals having reached ages of 2200 years, but other trees lay claim to the record of the oldest. However, it *is* the tallest species of tree in the world, growing from 80 to 325 feet in height, with a trunk 8 to 26 feet in diameter. The current champion measures over 379 feet.

< 8 >

< Secret Voices from the Forest >

Because these trees are so tall, the treetop needles are exposed to drier heat than the needles of branches below the dense canopy. In compensation, redwoods grow treetop needles with tight spikes that have very little evaporative surface, and are thereby able to conserve more moisture. The lower branches produce flat needles, which catch more light through the thick canopy.

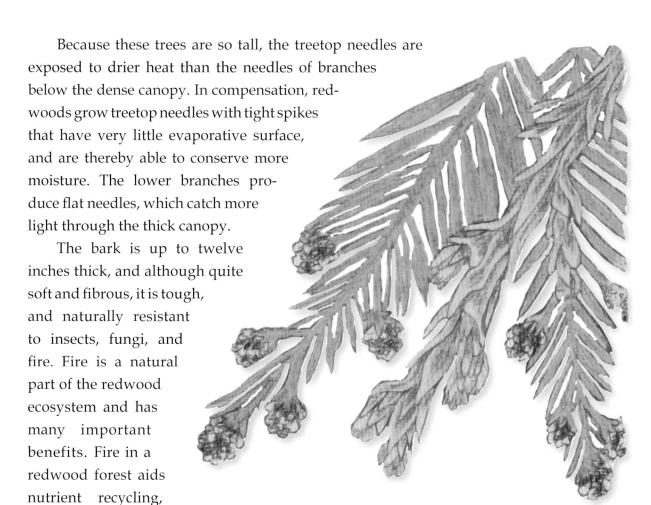

The bark is up to twelve inches thick, and although quite soft and fibrous, it is tough, and naturally resistant to insects, fungi, and fire. Fire is a natural part of the redwood ecosystem and has many important benefits. Fire in a redwood forest aids nutrient recycling, clears the understory, controls forest insects and diseases, and prepares the soil for seeds.

Amazingly, these huge trees have no taproots. Instead, their root system is composed of shallow, wide-spreading lateral roots that extend over one hundred feet from the base, intertwining with the roots of other redwoods. When a tree is inundated with silt from flooding, and the roots are buried under more soil, the tree adapts by growing new roots on top of the old, which then become anchors against the wind.

About fifty "albino" redwoods (mutant individuals which do not manufacture chlorophyll) are known to exist, reaching heights of up to sixty-six feet. These trees survive as parasites, obtaining food by grafting their root systems with those of normal trees. While similar mutations occur sporadically in other conifers, no cases are known of such individuals surviving to maturity in any other conifer species.

< Northern Pacific Coast : Temperate Rain Forest : Coastal Redwood >

Coastal Redwood Companions

California Red-legged Frog
Fetid Adder's Tongue
Helvella Acetabulum
Northwest Salamander

Tiger Lily
Harlequin Duck
Huckleberry
Pine White Butterfly
Redwood Sorrel

Vine Maple
Western Pond Turtle
Dall's Porpoise
Western Bleeding Heart

Banana Slug
Elegant Cat's Ears
Purple Finch
Sword Fern
Pine Marten

Rooted all to the same rock
are we many or one; many
or all of one regard?
Axe and fire;
fire and axe;
even to the last, listen
to the long work.

Does time feel
its own passing?
Can a whisper
take a hundred years?
Do the wet ocean winds
know where they come from or why
they are still
here?

What if air
is a dream and nothing
can be named, and by the slow upward
layering of height
we brushed against stars?

FACTS ABOUT SOME COASTAL REDWOOD COMPANIONS

Banana Slug

The Pacific banana slug is the second largest species of terrestrial slug in the world, growing nearly ten inches long. It has a single lung which opens externally via a breathing pore on its upper back.

At one time the slugs were blamed for damage done to redwood seedlings, but a later study proved the slugs would rather eat cardboard than a redwood seedling. Rather than doing damage, they instead eat other small plants in the environment that are the redwood's competitors.

In 1986, UC Santa Cruz students voted via referendum to make the banana slug their official college mascot—their reaction to over-the-top "competitive spirit" exhibited at most American universities.

The bright yellow mollusk, found in the campus's redwood forest, had been the unofficial mascot for several years, but there was a brief attempt to replace the banana slug with the sea lion, thought by the chancellor a more "dignified" animal. After five years, the student population's overwhelmingly pro-slug opinion prevailed, and the slug's status was made official. In May of 2004, *Reader's Digest* named the Sammy the Slug the best college mascot.[1]

< 12 >

Huckleberry

The red huckleberry is a common, edible shrub found in the coastal redwood community. The huckleberry has a place in archaic English slang, generally thought to mean, "the suitable person for the job."

The word was in usage as early as the mid-1600s, apparently a corruption of "hurtleberry," a common name for the European blueberry. After years of mispronunciation by the early colonists, the name stuck.

As huckleberries are relatively diminutive, the name came to mean "a tiny amount" or "a negligible thing or person." Mark Twain used the word more than once, first as the name of his famous character from *Huckleberry Finn*, first published in 1884, and then as a disparaging term in *A Connecticut Yankee in King Arthur's Court* in 1889.

As a metaphor for something very small, the huckleberry also appeared in phrases such as "to bet a huckleberry to a persimmon," to indicate an inconsequential amount. However, the term could also signify something unique, as in the phrase "the only huckleberry on the bush."[2]

< Secret Voices from the Forest >

Dall's Porpoise

The Dall's porpoise is the fastest of the small cetaceans, sometimes traveling at speeds up to 35 mph. It loves to bowride alongside fast-moving vessels, appearing suddenly at the bow, and disappearing just as quickly.

It often moves back and forth at great speed with jerky movements, creating a characteristic spray known as a "roostertail," which creates a hollow airspace in the water that allows the porpoise to continue breathing while swimming.

It has similar coloration as the orca, black with large, oval-shaped white sides and white underbellies. The species differs from other porpoises in that it prefers deep water and the open ocean. It may come closer to land, but if it does, it typically stays close to deep-water canyons. Dall's porpoises are found only in the north Pacific, ranging from Baja California north to Alaska and the Bering Sea and across into Japanese waters, seemingly confined to colder waters with temperatures less than 60 degrees F.

Tiger Lily

There are many species of true lilies native to North America, and several of them share the name "tiger lily." *Lilium columbianum* is a native lily that occurs in open woods and forest openings from southern British Columbia in Canada south to northern California and east to Idaho and Nevada in the USA.

An old legend from Korea tells about a hermit who saved the life of a tiger by removing an arrow from its body. The tiger was very grateful and wanted their friendship to last forever. When the tiger died, the hermit used his powers to turn the beast into the tiger lily flower, so they could be together. But one day a flood came, the hermit drowned, and his body was washed away. After that, Tiger Lily spread everywhere searching for its friend.

Harlequin Duck

The Harlequin Duck is a small sea duck, spending most of the year on the ocean and only traveling inland to breed. Harlequin Ducks prefer turbulent water. They breed and nest on remote, fast-flowing mountain streams, where their ability to swim and feed among the boulders of a raging river is unmatched.

They winter close to shore, feeding in raging surf or relaxing on rocks along rugged and exposed rocky coastlines. Migrating only short distances, Harlequin Ducks move from the coast inland and back again. They are relatively tame and can be approached closely in many areas.

Their name comes from a character of traditional Italian comedy and pantomime, the harlequin, who appeared in costumes made of multicolored triangular patches, and is a reference to the duck's brightly colored feathers of blue-gray, with markings of black, white, grey, and orange.

Sword Fern

Western sword fern is an evergreen that is abundant in western North America, particularly along the Pacific coast. The dark green fronds of this fern grow to nearly six feet. Its favored habitat is the understory of moist coniferous forests, at low elevations. The western sword fern has been found to be difficult or impossible to grow in the eastern part of the continent.

The sword fern is a member of a large plant group known as the *Pteridophyta*, consisting of all the other ferns, as well as horsetails and club mosses. Pteridophytes are plants with roots, stems and leaves, but no flowers or seeds, and reproduce by means of spores.

< 14 >

Mosses, horsetails and ferns were the dominant land-plant species during the Carboniferous Period, from about 354 to 290 million years ago. They reached monstrous sizes, as large as present-day trees. Analysis of air bubbles found in fossilized amber containing some of these species caused some scientists to speculate that the growth of megaflora, as well as megafauna, was due to much higher levels of oxygen and greater atmospheric pressure on Earth at that time. Today, these plants are generally much, much smaller, except in some tropical and subtropical places, where ferns can still reach quite large sizes.

As the climate began to go through drastic changes, becoming much drier, the gigantic ferns, horsetails, and club mosses began to die off en masse. Subjected to pressure and heat for millions of years, the layers compressed into the coal and oil deposits that we now use for fuel. The term "carboniferous" was coined to describe the rich deposits of coal that occur in England. These deposits of coal also occur throughout northern Europe, Asia, and mid-western and eastern North America.

David Suzuki, in his book, *Tree: A Life Story*, relates an incident from the mid-nineteenth century in one of England's coal digs. A fossil club moss from the carboniferous period was

< Secret Voices from the Forest >

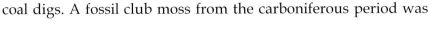

exposed, whose trunk, before the branches started, was thirty-nine feet long and three feet in diameter at the base. No one had ever seen anything like it before, as club mosses today are tiny plants, and scientists were called in to examine it. It showed, without a doubt, that the source of the heat energy released when these fuels are burned originally comes from the sun.[3]

Today, research into using algae as a biofuel, even a food source, is well underway. In 2009, two commercial airlines made test flights, using algae-based biofuel, with great success, getting slightly better mileage than petroleum-based jet fuel.[4]

Northwest Salamander

Northwestern salamanders are found on moist forest floors. They are difficult to find during the day, as they find cover under rotted logs and forest litter. They typically live below the surface for much of the year, and emerge on rainy nights in the fall and spring to breed, laying their eggs in still or slow-moving water.

The northwest salamander is one of only a few salamanders that retain gills into adulthood. Some also achieve sexual maturity while still in the larval stage; this characteristic seems to increase with altitude.[5]

Elegant Cat's Ears

Calochortus is a smaller group, or *genus*, of the Lily family. It includes Mariposa and globe lilies, fairy lanterns, cat's ears and star tulips. The word *Calochortus* is derived from the Greek and means "beautiful grass." Of the seventy species in this genus, twenty-eight are native to California. Like other lilies, its flower is arranged in multiples of three. The elegant cat's ears is an inhabitant of the moist, cool coniferous woodlands of the coastal forests.

Although the bulbs of many species of lilies were eaten by American Indians, and later by Mormon settlers during their first couple of winters in Utah, many species are poisonous and can even cause kidney failure in household pets, especially cats.

‹ Northern Pacific Coast : Temperate Rain Forest : Coastal Redwood ›

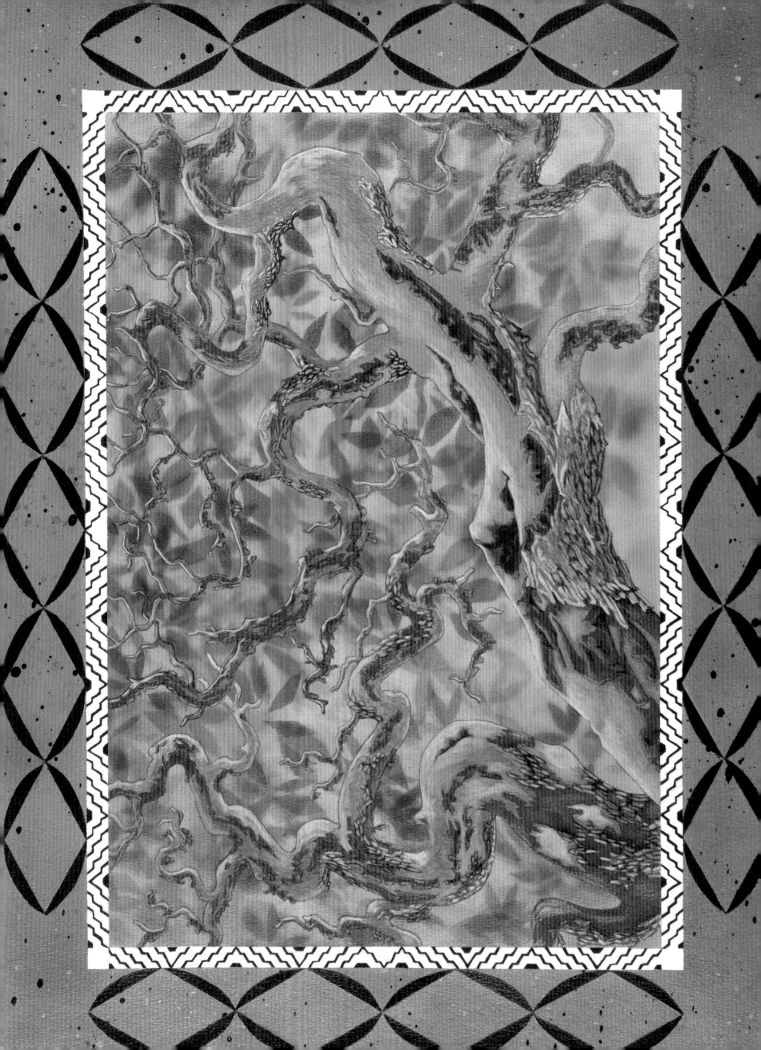

REFLECTIONS ON VISION

What Madrone Can Yell You About Itself

Look at the beautiful reds, oranges, and greens of my bark—they show up brightly against the dark green of the surrounding pines, spruces and firs. By being remarkable, I make the other trees of the forest more noticeable, and thereby more appreciated.

As a result, the forest becomes more than a uniform mass of unvaried scenery, easily ignored. It appears as another dimension, in which misty images swirl and beckon in not-quite-recognizable patterns that hint of a possible future hidden beneath surfacing dreams.

I am proud of my uniqueness. My process of manifesting *Vision* can provide a view into a realm of peace and calm, a dimension that troubles, mental conflict and anguish cannot touch, a dimension in which there is a sense of possibility and hope.

Life and relation are changeable and unpredictable. In the ebb and flow of my interactions, it may not seem that I accomplish anything of consequence, but I am constantly attempting to absorb the energy of other forms to comprehend their essence. It is a deep way of seeing. By doing so, I become *more*, allowing new possibilities to arise.

≺ 17 ≻

By encouraging my branches to twist and turn as they will, I illustrate that making sudden changes is an effective response to the challenges of happenstance. Sometimes it is best to keep your immediate thoughts and reactions concealed. In so doing, it may be possible for you to transform adversity into opportunity.

Madrone's Place in the World

It loves being near the ocean, where the air is warm and invites change. It embraces the fog, which creeps in and lies heavily upon the forest floor. Fog gives personal boundaries to each tree—a mirror that shows the singularity of "I" for a brief second of joyful self-awareness, and then dissolves again into the endless dance of form.

Madrone is a manifestation of the paradox of *self* and *selflessness*. While it is a member of the Heath Family of trees and shrubs, which personifies humility—*conspicuous* humility—it is relatively showy. In spite of this, its unique gift is to know that The Jester is the most humble one of all, knowing his true place in the universe is to be a blink in the eye of God.

While this species of tree has only a tiny part to play in the life of the planet, by making color from the elements, it makes the world brighter and more interesting with its presence.

Madrone has learned that the planet Earth is crumbling all the time. It says that Time may be an illusion, but it is an illusion shared by all, so living will always retain its fascination. To keep ahead of the curve of Time, you should acquire wisdom, which will pass with you into your next form. Perception is everything, and, as knowledge of space and time is relative to the position of the observer, illusion to one is truth to another.

Consider the wolf: although the animal's feet may be planted in insoluble reality, when it is witnessed, its image changes to accommodate the needs of the watcher. As a result, it has become a protagonist in the pageant of fear and blame of the *other*.

Madrone's Message for Us

Nothing happens in a vacuum. There must be concurrence for movement. But cooperation requires wisdom—seeing the needs of all, and knowing when new circumstances require methods be altered. The climate is not the only thing that is changing.

The human race creates complications, and sometimes acceleration of inevitable events. It seems to be the embodiment of choice, but is really many free-floating bits of protoplasm in the ocean of the universe, each dreaming about what it can become. We all pass endlessly through the star systems of our own bodies—universes within universes—seeing everything from the spiral motion of an ever-changing perspective.

< 18 >

The quality of Vision manifests in humans as a problem that requires a solution, as well as a *solution* to that problem. It is your nature to emphasize possibilities that will improve your lives or give you comfort. Sometimes that need for comfort moves in directions that give discomfort to others, so your challenge is to be aware of consequences—not simply to yourself, but to all other life forms.

Your contribution to the life of the planet is velocity. You influence the natural forces of the Earth to move with greater rapidity. There may be good in this, in ways we cannot see now.

Everything works together, whether each of us sees it happening or not. In the future we will all *comprehend* this.

Open yourself up to living, as the only real fate is change.

< Secret Voices from the Forest >

CHRONICLES

The Pacific madrone is a tree that screams "Color!" It is broadleaved and evergreen, with a picturesque form of twisting branches and flaking bark that peels off in large, thin scales. Once the outer bark is shed, what remains has a smooth, polished appearance and varies in color from a fissured dark brown to a deep red. Younger branches and trunks are orange, and stems range from green to chartreuse.

‹ Northern Pacific Coast : Temperate Rain Forest : Pacific Madrone ›

Extending from British Columbia through most of California, it occurs mainly in the Puget Sound, Oregon Coast Range and California Coast Ranges. Because of its bright summer berries, as well as its often orange-colored bark, it has been called "the Strawberry Tree." Amongst the trees of the Pacific Northwest, the madrone tree is often confused with the manzanita tree because of the similar coloring of the bark.

It has thick, dark green, glossy leaves that stay on the tree for two years. The tree is never without leaves, as the old leaves — by then colored bright orange and red — only drop off after a new crop of leaves has fully grown. The height of a madrone can range from 16 to 130 feet, and under ideal conditions it can be as much as 8 feet thick at the base of the trunk.

Although part of the rainforest system, the Pacific madrone reaches greatest abundance on hotter, drier sites that are unfavorable to conifer growth. In Canada, it is the only native broad-leaved evergreen tree, and it rarely extends inland more than five miles. You will find Pacific madrone to be more abundant on rocky coastal sites that are also somewhat dry, as well as exposed or wooded slopes and canyons below 5000 ft.

Pacific madrone is restricted to areas where the ocean winters are mild; however, temperature and moisture conditions vary considerably throughout its range. It can be damaged or even killed if it endures long or severe periods of frost, and it has moderate to low shade tolerance, which varies depending on latitude. As the trees age, the need for light increases, and older trees require top light for survival.

Under natural conditions, the madrone depends on intermittent fires to reduce the amount of shade produced by surrounding conifers. Pacific madrone generally has low resistance to fire, because of its thin bark, but mature trees can survive, and can regenerate more rapidly after fire than the Douglas-firs which are often nearby. They also produce a very large number of seeds, which sprout following fire.

In spring, deer eat the blossoms, and what the deer leave behind, the bees pollinate; then hummingbirds feed on the nectar. From the pollinated flower follows the red fruit, food for many types of birds and other animals, such as American Robins, Cedar Waxwings,

< 20 >

< Secret Voices from the Forest >

Band-tailed Pigeons, Varied Thrushes, Montezuma Quail, mule deer, raccoons, ring-tailed cats, squirrels, and bears. It is also important as a nesting site for many birds, and in mixed woodland, it seems to be a favorite building material for nests.

The Salish of Vancouver Island used the bark and leaves to brew medicines to treat colds, tuberculosis, and bladder infections, and to prevent conception. The bark was used for tanning or dyeing, and small pieces of the wood were used for tools and eating utensils. Curved limbs could be used to build doorways and roofs for dwellings.

In the myths of the Salish, a human-like form of pitch enjoyed fishing, but needed to return to shore before it got too hot. One day he was too late getting back to shore and melted from the heat. Several trees rushed to get the pitch for themselves—the first was Douglas Fir, which absorbed most of it, Grand Fir got a little, and the Madrone got none at all—which is why they say it still has no pitch.

On the British Columbia West Coast, the Salish Nation calls the Madrone tree their "Tree of Knowledge," as they say it knows how to find the sun, twisting branches back on themselves to avoid shade and reach the sunlight.

According to the Great Flood legends of several tribes in the northwest, the Madrone helped people to survive by becoming an anchor on top of a mountain that held their canoes steady and kept them from drifting away. It is still not burnt as firewood, in memory of the refuge and protection it provided them long ago.[6]

 < 21 >

Madrone is considered "most sacred," a symbol of the balance between darkness and light, its webbed roots holding the splintered earth together. The myths warn that should the madrone disappear, the planet would fly apart and be completely destroyed. This is probably from the observation that madrone trees contribute to cliff and bluff stability. The roots go down to the bedrock in search for water, and if the trees are removed, bluffs over the water may become more susceptible to landslides.

< Northern Pacific Coast : Temperate Rain Forest : Pacific Madrone >

Pacific Madrone Companions

Craterellus cornucopioides
Mountain Goat
Underwing Moth
Wild Ginger

Western Boreal Toad
Firecracker Flower
10-Lined June Beetle
Salmonberry
Western Meadowlark

California Sea Lion
White Rhododendron
Horsetail Fern
Northern Alligator Lizard

Blue Anemone
Pacific Orangetip Butterfly
Cascara Buckthorn
Red Crossbill
Oregon Grape

fog moves inland, bringing from
the seas submersion and the sinuous
progress of swimming as it furls and unfurls,
mounting the still-shaded cliffs, penetrating
the wooded hills beyond, closing off steep clefts,
rolling into rooty hollows where it mingles with
mist lifting lightly from small pools and fern-
covered streams, and moves on to fill the dimmed
accidental avenues, crowding the silent portals of
trees, emerging among them as shifting densities
which evaporate into half-completed vaults,
condense in cool droplets between flaking and living
bark, sink down like a weight of blank dream, always
moving, weaving . . .
—but is there something else which also breathes
and drips from wetted leaves, also slips effortlessly
aside from bole and bough, unbound, thinning
suddenly to a shaft of silvered haze, wondering do
    the birds, pursuing their songs from branch to
      unseen branch, adore, like this—like *this*!—
        their own unwitnessed wings?

FACTS ABOUT SOME PACIFIC MADRONE COMPANIONS

Underwing Moth

species Catocala faustina allusa

Usually nocturnal, the underwing moth is named for its brightly colored hindwings, which are only displayed in flight. The distinctive orange, yellow, pink, red, or white markings vary greatly among the thousands of species of this moth. It spends its days resting against trees or stumps, with its forewings open, as the shades of patterned gray and brown look so much like bark that the moth is completely camouflaged. Experiments have shown that different species will select the tree whose bark will help them increase the degree to which they are camouflaged. The genus name, *catocala*, is a combination of two Greek words, *kato* (behind), and *kalos* (beautiful).

Horsetail Fern

The horsetail is a remarkable plant for many reasons. Four hundred million years ago, its descendants were huge plants that grew ten feet high. It is a close relative of the fern, and also an ancient non-flowering member of the flora kingdom.

Horsetail is a perennial, with hollow stems and shoots that pop apart in sections. As the plant dries, silica crystals that form in the stems and branches look like feathery tails and give the plant a scratching effect. No plant is more concentrated in silica than horsetail, and it was used by American Indians to clean utensils, and the early pioneers as a "scouring pad" to clean pots and pans, and to polish their pewter. This was an even more convenient practice due to the fact that horsetail prefers to grow near water.

In its use as a medicinal herb, it is sought after for its silicic acid and silica content. This use dates back at least to ancient Roman and Greek medicine. Herbalists of those times believed in the wound-healing properties of the plant and used it to heal ulcers, stop bleeding, and even help kidney conditions. In modern herbal medicine, it is applied for treating rheumatism and calcium insufficiency symptoms, but very few studies have been done on horsetail's effect in humans.

Western Meadowlark

This familiar bird is a colorful member of the blackbird family, which includes blackbirds, orioles, cowbirds, and grackles. The Western Meadowlark is an open-country bird, nesting on the ground. Males commonly use fence posts as perches while singing. Their song is often heard on movie soundtracks even when the setting is far from the bird's range.

The males will sing to claim a breeding territory, and usually have as many as three mates at the same time. The females do all the incubation and brooding, and most of the feeding of the young.

It is the state bird of Kansas, Montana, Nebraska, North Dakota, Oregon and Wyoming. Only the Northern Cardinal is the state bird of more states. One of the two species, Western or Eastern, may be found in meadows and fields from one coast to the other, and from the Canadian prairie to Mexico.

Physically, the two species are very difficult to tell apart, but the songs of the two vary greatly. The two species are so similar that it was not until 1844 that Audubon noticed the difference and named the western bird *neglecta* because it had been overlooked for so long.

An Indian legend of the Pacific Northwest tells of how Meadowlark and Coyote made a rope of twisted hazel shoots and stretched it across the Willamette River, trying to make a waterfall. They stopped where Salem is today, and Meadowlark said, "Let's make it here." Since Coyote did not understand Meadowlark's language, he turned some animals into rocks, instead of making waterfalls. They walked on down the river, stopping where Oregon City is now. This time Meadowlark used sign language, and Coyote understood what she wanted. They pulled the rope tight across the river, and Coyote used his powers to turn the rope into a rock. The river then poured over the rock, which is how Willamette Falls were created.[7]

Cascara Buckthorn

Chitticum, in the Chinook language, cascara buckthorn is the largest species of buckthorn. It is native to western North America from southern British Columbia south to central California, and inland to western Montana.

The dried and aged bark of this tree has been used continually for at least 1,000 years by both native and immigrant Americans as a laxative, commercially called "Cascara Sagrada," but old-timers call it "*chitticum* bark." *Chitticum* is "shit come," in Chinook. The bark is comes mostly from wild trees. Over-harvesting in the mid-1900s eliminated mature trees near many settled areas. Once stripped from the tree, the bark is aged for about one year to make its effect milder. Fresh cut, dried bark causes vomiting and violent diarrhea.

Cascara Sagrada was accepted in medical practice in the United States in 1877, and by 1890 had replaced the berries of the european buckthorn as a commonly used laxative. It was the principal ingredient in many commercial, over-the-counter laxatives in North American pharmacies until 2002, when the U.S. Food and Drug Administration issued a final rule banning the use of aloe and cascara sagrada as laxative ingredients in over-the-counter drug products.

Firecracker Flower

Dichelostemma ida-maia is a native of Northwest California and Southwest Oregon. This bright crimson, tube-shaped member of the lily family hangs in clusters of six to thirteen flowers, off a tall single stem. According to the *Audubon Society Field Guide to North American Wildflowers*, this charming wildflower's species name honors the niece of a stagecoach driver, who showed the plant to an early collector. Her name was Ida May.

< 26 >

California Sea Lion

The familiar circus seal is typically a California sea lion. They are known for their intelligence and playfulness, and adapt easily to man-made environments. They have been trained by the U.S. Navy for military operations, such as detecting underwater land mines and the recovery of equipment. In the wild, the California sea lion is a sleek animal, faster than any other sea lion or seal, reaching speeds of 25 mph.

California sea lions live along the rocky Pacific Ocean coastlines of western North America. They are very social animals, and great numbers "haul out," at the same time, forming colonies. They lie together, or on top of one another, on sandy beaches, marina docks, jetties, and buoys. They sometimes float in proximity to each other in groups called "rafts."

Sea lions have vocal cords. They are one of the most vocal mammals, communicating with each other via barks,

< Secret Voices from the Forest >

growls, and grunts. Mothers and pups call to each other, each identifying their own. Sea lions also communicate visually, with postural displays particularly related to territory and mating.

Mothers and pups also recognize each other by smell and sight. As females normally behave extremely aggressively towards pups that are not theirs, the accepted belief has been that an orphan is rarely adopted. However, marine biologist Ramona Flatz, from Arizona State University, has recently done some studies that show a growing number of adoptions amongst certain populations of female sea lions. She feels this may be the work of people. Increased tourism, which can disturb young mothers and make them leave their pups, may account for the increased number of adoptions that are occurring.[8]

The sea lion's ancient ancestors, like those of whales and dolphins, lived on land. Their front flippers had all the same major bones as do the forelimbs of land mammals, but they have been modified for swimming. The "arm" bones are now shortened, and the flippers are like our hands, with the "fingers" lengthened by extensions of cartilage at the tips of the finger bones, decreasing in length as they near the body. The five digits in the hind limbs are all roughly the same length. On land, a sea lion can rotate its hind flippers underneath the body, giving sea lions the ability to walk and stand on all fours. In the water, a sea lion extends its front flippers in an up-and-down, wing-like motion to propel itself through the water, and the hind flippers are used to help steer.

Long-tailed Wild Ginger

< 27 >

This tiny, ground-hugging plant is found from British Columbia south through Washington and Oregon to central California, and from the Coast Range east to western Montana, below 5000 feet. It occurs mostly in deciduous woodland or coniferous forests.

Wild ginger is unrelated to the ginger plant commonly used today for cooking, but because of its aroma and taste, the American Indians used it as a culinary herb.

Wild ginger has been used in traditional medicine by the American Indians, as well as by practitioners of Traditional Oriental Medicine, for treating many conditions. It was also used as a stimulant, and as a salve base for treating cuts and bruises. It was thought to protect those who ate spoiled meat or food that might be poisoned or have some sort of a spell cast on it. The plant has been shown to have certain antimicrobial properties, and the accounts of it being used to prevent sickness from eating questionable meat are numerous.

< Northern Pacific Coast : Temperate Rain Forest : Pacific Madrone >

⪻ OLD GROWTH FOREST ⪼

REFLECTIONS ON MEMORY

What Old Growth Can Tell You About Itself

*M*emory is touching the depths of the Earth to discover where She has been. It is calling to the winds as they pass, to hear about the changes they have witnessed.

Animals know what they must do to flourish, as it is written partially in their genes. But that is true of all matter, really. The earth slowly renews, arising from the dissolution of its many forms, as do the mountains and seas. Although rock and water are completely different life forms, they are the source of all others, through the continual rearrangement of their chemical elements.

As motionless as I must appear to those who experience time passing as quickly as you, within me there is constant metamorphosis taking place. It begins with the very tiniest particles of life, then radiates outward. I am the everlasting mutation of forms. Life moves into death, as death is merely a phase of life.

Wait, and all things will come to you. Patience is hard to learn. The nature of our kind of life is to strive, to long to be somewhere else, to be something more than what we are. But the lesson is well worth learning, as peace and clarity of mind are the rewards.

I do not regard the passage of Time the same as you. We have a difference in perception. Imagine that you are swimming. The body of water appears to be a single object that you can penetrate, but it actually consists of many, many small beings, acting in concert. It is their nature to part as you pass. Conditions you are designed to notice—changes in weather, movement of animals, for instance—seem to us to come and go very quickly.

The equivalent experience for those in the plant world is the observance of each small part—the passage of water through cells, the extending of stem, branch, and flower, the falling of individual flakes of snow. It is an effort for us to see as you do, although not impossible.

Because of this, I can tell you that the actions of your species are more in harmony than you know, like the drops of water in the ocean. The symphony of life on this planet has many unheard movements. The Future is not yet fixed.

Old Growth's Place in the World

Old Growth is a repository of the Memory of what has passed. As we share its experience, Old Growth assures us that nothing will ever be forgotten. What is important is the continuation and intermingling of life. Many beings are moving together into islands for protection. Nothing wants to die, particularly alone or in an alien environment. But it also shows us that the Essence of what fills and connects the spaces between forms is the greatest source of life that exists. As you feel the mist come from the ocean, you can begin to understand that there is always something larger than yourself. It seems that we are all islands, emanating from the core of the planet—its soul on display.

Old Growth also knows that there are other forms of life that inhabit these connecting spaces. In the deep, hot places of the earth, there are those who make, or rather, *become* metal. They are sometimes forced to the surface, but as this is not a hospitable environment for them; they soon solidify. In the spaces above the surface of the earth, and in the waters, there are intelligences that watch and remember, which could be called Angels. These beings have occasionally been seen, and thus are the source of the mythical creatures of legend.

Old Growth can direct us towards an experience of the soft, mysterious effects of light. As the sun moves overhead, or the moon grows full, these effects are in constant flux. As each moment passes, color takes on new and different variations, vibrating, refracting, seemingly alive in its response to these changing elements.

Old Growth is like an ant colony. All its parts work together in harmony, and in so doing change the makeup of the earth. Even the tiniest creature can have big effects.

The chatter in the wind is that a time of conclusion is coming. We must be generous with our energy, so it will pass into another form without the burden of fear. Old Growth's place is a reminder, to those who are observant, of this: all things, no matter how mighty or limitless they seem, pass.

< 30 >

Old Growth's Message for Us

Memory manifests in humanity through curiosity, through the desire to know. We have tools. They are an extension of different parts of our bodies. Language and writing, history and science are outreaches of the capacities of our brains. For each new question, we make new instruments that help us learn.

We can use these tools to learn more about the Earth and her past. As we do so, we are able to put our own place in the world in perspective. Although our individual encounters with time are relatively short, we have the ability to discover the past knowledge and experiences of our species, and make record of it in our own unique way. Knowing the past engenders respect, and allows for wiser choices.

We have a geometric approach to life, and are capable of seeing something from many perspectives at once, making each of those vantage points manifest more completely. But, as we see the varying paths to take, we have, through our acquired memories, the *ability* to make wise choices. Our lesson here is to learn to make those choices.

Old Growth's wish for our future is that we are able to organically incorporate the memory of the planet and others who dwell on it into our own collective knowledge.

< Secret Voices from the Forest >

CHRONICLES

< 31 >

An old growth can be defined as any forest that has been standing, with minimal disturbance, for a period of 100 to 500 years. The forest referred to here is that of the Pacific Northwest of North America, which has stood undisturbed since the retreat of the last ice age, some 11,000 years ago. Although much reduced in area from its original expanse, in volume, it is the most massive forest on earth.

To be called old growth, a forest must exhibit all of these characteristics at the same time:
• Large and old live trees, and trees of mixed ages in a multilayered canopy. New trees regenerate at different times from each other, because each one of them receives a different amount of light. Trees in younger forests have similar ages, because their regeneration began immediately after the preceding forest was eliminated by, for instance, fire, climate change,

< Northern Pacific Coast : Temperate Rain Forest : Old Growth Forest >

or logging. Forest canopy gaps are essential in creating and maintaining mixed-age stands. Openings are a result of tree death due to wind, smaller fires and tree diseases.

• Large, standing dead trees, called *snags*. A dead tree may remain standing for over two hundred years, providing food and habitat for many types of organisms. Bird species, such as woodpeckers, need snags to find food, as snags are full of insects that feed on rotting wood. The spotted owl is known to need standing snags in which to nest.

• Large fallen trees. Lying on the forest floor, they help to hold the soil in place, becoming food and shelter for dozens of species of insects, birds and mammals. Fallen timber creates smaller microhabitats on the forest floor, and puts rich organic matter directly into the soil. As they decay over hundreds of years, these fallen trees may become nurse logs, themselves providing a base for seedling trees to grow. Other fallen trees lie in streams, regulating the passage of water, and creating habitat that will harbor many future generations of insects and bacteria, ultimately the supporting ecosystem for many fish, such as coho salmon and cutthroat trout.

The fall of individual trees opens up gaps in the main canopy layer, allowing light to penetrate, thereby creating favorable conditions for photosynthesis in the understory. The understory in an old growth system is more developed than that of the understory in a secondary growth system.

Much of the surface terrain of an old growth forest consists of pits and mounds. Pits are caused when a tree falls, through natural causes, pulling the roots up, along with large chunks of soil. Mounds are the result of decaying fallen trees. Each is a unique habitat, and supports a different group of organisms. They both help to make the topography of the forest floor very irregular.

Because they have remained undisturbed for such a long period of time, old growth forests contain a much more varied community of plants and animals than a secondary growth system. They depend on the unique environmental conditions present, and some of them are rare or even endangered. If a system is not fragmented, it can support very large animals that require space to roam or hunt, such as elk and bear.

< 32 >

< Secret Voices from the Forest >

Old growth forests are a haven for species of plants that are unable to thrive or easily regenerate in younger forests. They may also contain previously unidentified plant species, some of which could be developed into new medicines, as has been seen with several plants from the tropical rainforest.

Because they store large amounts of carbon in wood, soil humus and peat, the old growth forests help to control the world's climate. As the forests are removed, the carbon is released as carbon dioxide or methane, which many feel will increase the risk of rapid and irreversible global climate change. Studies of soils in some of the world's undisturbed areas have found that these carbon stores can be bound up for 1,000 years or more before they are released naturally.

Conifers are the dominant species in these forests, and the four main species of those are Douglas fir, Sitka spruce, western hemlock, and western redcedar. Douglas fir is the second tallest tree in the world, after coastal redwood, and Sitka spruce is the third tallest. They are all long-lived, many exceeding 1000 years of age.

As the forest is cut down, the remaining, often relatively small patches of trees become isolated and fragmented. Within them, the populations of many species of plants and animals suffer from loss of habitat, and are often, in the case of large predators, unable to survive at all.[9]

In *The Fragmented Forest*, the late Professor Larry D. Harris proposes the Island Biogeographic Theory, a system of greater and smaller islands linked by corridors that extend the effective range of species threatened by confinement and lack of genetic diversity. In April of 2010, a bill was introduced into Congress, H.R. 5101—The Wildlife Corridors Conservation Act of 2010—to implement this idea. To date, the future of this bill remains uncertain, as does the future of the forest itself.[10]

‹ Northern Pacific Coast : Temperate Rain Forest : Old Growth Forest ›

Old Growth Forest Companions

Ceanothus Silkmoth
Liverwort
Agoseris
Red-backed Tree Vole

Elegant Jacob's Ladder
Sitka Black-tailed Deer
Yellow Skunk Cabbage
Black-capped Chickadee
Indian Pipe

Pacific Bayberry
Sockeye Salmon
Pacific Giant Salamander
Toyon

Western Spotted Skunk
Fringe Caps
Western Banded Glowworm
Jack-O-Lantern Shelf Fungus
Northern Spotted Owl

The base of the great tree,
    gnawed, hollowed, split and strained
by age and storm,
fails at last in the final wind,
splinters, cracks,
and all that towering weight above
topples, slowly at first,
even majestically, then
crashes like a slain king
through the giving arms of its kind,
down to the dark floor.

But in the shocked, reverberant
hush, a new light
is also descending, touching
exposed leaves, quickening seeds.
In a hundred years another tree,
having won the race of sun
and shade, will stand here again,
strong roots strongly entwined
in its own ancestral soil.

FACTS ABOUT SOME OLD GROWTH COMPANIONS

Spotted Owl

The Northern Spotted Owl is most often associated with mature and old growth forests, because these forests have greater than 40% to 70% canopy cover. Spotted Owls have a large home range, covering from 1,000 to 14,000 acres. They do not build their own nests, but rely on sites such as trees and snags with cavities or broken tops, and platforms associated with abandoned nests and debris accumulations.

Spotted Owls can live to be seventeen years old, but the quality of their habitat is of great importance. They are very territorial and cannot tolerate disturbance of their habitat. They need high, open canopies in which they are able to fly between and underneath the trees. They don't usually cross clear-cut or brushy areas. Monogamous breeders, a pair of spotted owls requires 2,000-5,000 acres of contiguous forest. If breeding fails, they rarely attempt again.

These birds hunt mostly at night. They wait on their perches, swoop silently down on unsuspecting prey, and grasp it with their talons. They also capture prey in mid-air and from branches. Spotted owls' diet varies with location, but most often consists of flying squirrels, wood rats and tree voles.

< 36 >

Mountain Dandelion

Officially named orange agoseris, this flower is a member of the Daisy family, much like the common dandelion, which is the largest family of *vascular* plants. A vascular plant is one that uses a water-resistant channel—something like a straw—to convey fluids. An *avascular* plant, such as algae, mosses, and liverworts, which evolved earlier, is one that does not use these structures.

Distributed worldwide, we have derived many food substances from the Daisy family, including cooking oils, lettuce, sunflower seeds, artichokes, sweetening agents, and teas. Like the dandelion, it has great value as a culinary and medicinal herb, and is an important plant for bees and butterflies. Its deep taproot is able to bring up nutrients from hard earth, making it a pioneer plant and a good companion for weaker crops or those with shallow roots. It is also known to release ethylene gas when pollinated, which helps orchard fruit to ripen.

< Secret Voices from the Forest >

Sockeye Salmon

Sockeye salmon are born in fresh water, and spend up to four years there before migrating to the ocean, where they spend their adult years growing and taking on their distinctive color from the orange krill that is their diet. When it is time to spawn, they travel thousands of miles to return to the same freshwater system in which they were born. There they will spawn and die within a few weeks.

To several Indian tribes of the Northwest, salmon was one of the most important sources of food, and the fish itself was greatly esteemed. It was considered a race of people, consisting of five separate clans who lived in underwater communities.

In summer, when the Salmon People left their underwater lodges, traveling upstream to spawn, they would allow themselves to be caught in their fish form. This generous behavior was honored in the harvest rituals of the tribes, who performed salmon-welcoming ceremonies and returned the bones of the first salmon catch to the water so they could be born again. If willing, they might come back again to feed the People.[11]

Indian Pipe

< 37 >

Unlike most plants, the Indian pipe does not contain chlorophyll. Instead of generating energy from sunlight, it acts as a parasite on certain fungi that have a symbiotic relationship with trees. Since it is not dependent on sunlight, it can grow in very dark environments, such as the understory of a dense forest. It is sometimes completely white, but often has black flecks and a pale pink coloration, or it can also be a deep red.

One Indian legend tells how, a long time ago, all the tribes were peaceful and happy to share. There were no boundaries and no arguments. Then selfishness crept into the world, and the tribes began to argue. After one particularly long and bitter quarrel, the chiefs decided to meet in council to settle their differences. They solemnly smoked the peace pipe, but did not let go of their bitter words. After many days, the Great Spirit looked down at the old men sitting amid clouds of smoke, looking grey and tired. To teach them to only smoke the pipe of peace in earnest, he turned the old men there in council to small silvery gray flowers, with their heads bent down.

After the Great Spirit had changed the quarreling Indians into flowers and set them out in the forest, he noticed that the smoke from their pipes still hung heavy in the air above the place where the council had been. So he gathered up the smoke and draped it over the mountains as a reminder, until such time as all Men learn to live in peace together.[12]

< Northern Pacific Coast : Temperate Rain Forest : Old Growth Forest >

Pacific Giant Salamander

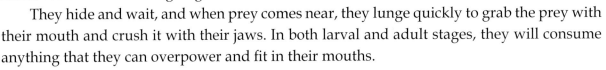

This amphibian is the largest terrestrial salamander in North America, sometimes growing to almost fourteen inches. The adult often never completely matures, retaining gills throughout its life, which can be as much as twenty-five years. While most salamanders are silent, the Pacific giant salamander is one of several salamanders that produces noise. It will emit a low-pitched croaky-sounding cry similar to that of a barking dog when threatened.

They hide and wait, and when prey comes near, they lunge quickly to grab the prey with their mouth and crush it with their jaws. In both larval and adult stages, they will consume anything that they can overpower and fit in their mouths.

Liverwort

Liverworts are typically small and are therefore often overlooked. They are most common in moist and tropical areas. Liverworts are more commonly found in moderate to deep shade, though desert species may tolerate direct sunlight and periods of total desiccation.

The first liverworts arose at the same time as green algae made its transition onto land, 400 million years ago. Liverworts are often referred to as "the simplest true plants." Instead of the familiar type of roots, liverworts anchor themselves with *rhizoids*, which are simple, one-celled extensions. As an avascular plant, they have almost no conductive tissues.

Because the plant resembled a human liver, it was once believed that liverworts cured diseases of the liver, hence the name. This archaic relationship of plant form to function was based in the "Doctrine of Signatures." This theory states that plants resembling various parts of the body can be used to treat ailments of that part of the body.

The concept was developed by Paracelsus (1491–1541) and published in his writings. During the first half of the sixteenth century, Paracelsus traveled throughout Europe, countries bordering the eastern Mediterranean Sea, and Egypt, treating people and experimenting with new plants in search of more treatments.

The doctrine of signatures was further spread by the writings of Jakob Böhme (1575–1624), who suggested that God marked objects with a sign, or "signature," of their function. A plant bearing parts that resembled human body parts, animals, or other objects were thought to have useful relevance to those parts, animals or objects.

Although the doctrine of signatures was formalized in early modern times, the

< 38 >

< Secret Voices from the Forest >

theme of natural objects' shapes having significance is a very old one and is not confined to Western thought. Since ancient times, the occasional resemblance of mandrake root to a human body has led to its being ascribed great significance and supernatural powers.

Nicholas Culpeper's *Complete Herbal* takes the doctrine of signatures as common knowledge, and its influence can still be detected in modern herbal lore. Modern scientists see the doctrine of signatures as superstition, and are as rejecting of the theory as modern doctors are of the healing properties of herbs. However, both herbalists and flower essence practitioners continue to find helpful hints in such connections.[13]

Ceanothus Silkmoth

This large, beautifully marked moth is found from British Columbia to Baja California. It is a member of the *Saturniidae* family, some of the largest insects alive today. The tropical Atlas moth, also of this family, can have a wingspan up to twelve inches. This family of moths is found all over the world, but their greatest species-diversity is in Mexico and the New World Tropics.

The moths in this family, and the domesticated silkmoth from the family *Bombycidae*, produce silk which has commercial application. Silk from the cocoons of the silk moth is not only used to make fabric, but is also used to make sutures for the medical industry.

At least seventy pounds of silk are produced each year, requiring nearly 10 billion pounds of mulberry leaves, the food of the domesticated silkmoth, and as many as 210,000 cocoons. Because the larva releases an enzyme to break down the fibers of the cocoon in order to emerge, the cocoons are boiled, both to kill the worm and to make the cocoons easier to unravel.

Most silkmoth caterpillars have hairy or spiny tubercules. One member of this family, the *Lonomia*, has spines that contain one of the most deadly toxins produced by any animal in the world. In the tropics, there are several reported deaths each year from contact with the *Lonomia* caterpillar.

The job of the caterpillar is to eat and turn into an adult; the job of the adult is to mate and reproduce. An adult female emerges with a complete set of mature ova. She then "calls" males by emitting pheromones, and generally will not fly until after she has mated. A male can detect these chemical signals up to a mile away and will fly several miles in one night to locate a female and mate with her.

The mouthparts of the adults of this butterfly are not functional and there is no digestive tract. Adults do not feed. The adult subsists on stored lipids acquired during the larval stage. As a result, the adult's lifespan is a week or less, once it has emerged from the pupa.

THE SACRED TREE

A belief common to both the tribes of the Celts and the American Indians was that of the Sacred Tree. The details are different, but the idea was similar, that this tree united the upper and lower regions, both the spiritual and the physical realms of the Earth.

The top of the tree was an over-world, where the Sky People dwelt. They were, variously, the star beings seen in the constellations, the godlike progenitors of human kind, or spirit forms who created and then dropped or threw down The People.

Animals seemed to exist already, and could talk and reason and bargain with the Sky People, and would sometimes be rewarded or punished with some physical characteristic—distinctive coloring, for instance—because of this intervention. Raven, Coyote, Turtle, and Bison are examples of this.

There was a middle realm in which humans lived, the physical world of day and work. What happened there was caused by, or a reflection of, the events and conditions of the other two worlds.

Last, or rather first, there was a lower region of sleep and dreams and ancestors. This place was seen as the source of life, and the place where all life returned when physical existence was over, to be reabsorbed by Death. The roots of the tree were in the lower region, recognizing that much of the motivation in our everyday lives and thought was unknowable in the light of day, but more powerful and basic than the wakeful mind.

The cultures holding these traditional beliefs lived in or near the great primeval forests, which were thousands of years old when humans first became unified into cultural groups, and the trees would have been seen as not only alive, but as conscious and aware.

In Europe, and the greater part of North America, these tremendous forests blanketed thousands of square miles, only broken up by bodies of water, the highest mountains, or regions of steppe. Many of these old trees had massive trunks, or lifted so high into the air that their tops could not be seen from the ground, so it was a completely plausible idea that trees could touch the heavens. There were no tall buildings, and no air travel, and the great trees would not have been cut down without fear of terrible retribution from the spirit of the land.

CHAPTER TWO

SOUTHERN PACIFIC COAST
MEDITERRANEAN CHAPARRAL AND
RIPARIAN WOODLANDS

rain on the coastal hills,
every toughened leaf
displays a fragile drop

≻≻≻≻≻≻≻≻≻≺≺≺≺≺≺≺≺

SOUTHERN PACIFIC COAST:
MEDITERRANEAN CHAPARRAL AND
RIPARIAN WOODLANDS

This climate zone is considered *temperate*. A temperate zone is either one of two belts of latitude between the Torrid Zone—that nearest to the equator—and the northern and southern frigid zones of the poles. It is a region characterized by mild, rainy winters and warm, dry summers, and is moderated by cold ocean currents offshore. The Mediterranean forest, woodlands, and shrub eco-regions are located along the western edges of continents, distributed between roughly thirty and forty degrees latitude. Chaparral regions lie between cool, lush belts of vegetation and areas of desert, either north or south of the equator. For the continent of North America, that includes southern California and northern Baja California.

Some theorize that areas of chaparral formed as a result of human habitation. These regions, with their comfortable year-round temperatures, became the permanent home to early civilizations and ever-increasing numbers of people. They cleared land for crops and herds. They cut down trees to build, cook, heat their homes and work with pottery and metals. The forests disappeared, and the topsoil, without the roots of trees to hold it in place, was eroded by wind and rain. The final factor would have been overgrazing, which would have depleted the soil of remaining nutrients, making it thin and desiccated, allowing the chaparral plants, which had always been there in small numbers, to take over.[1]

These plants have, over the centuries, become well adapted to the varying temperatures and poor soil of the region. Many trees are drought and fire resistant, and others have been dwarfed from constant exposure to poor soil, extreme climate changes, severe drought, and repeated wild fires.

Much of the woody vegetation in Mediterranean climate regions is *sclerophyll*, which means "hard-leaved" in Greek. Trees, such as the coastal and canyon live oaks, which have thick, succulent leaves covered with a waxy outside layer to retain moisture, are examples. Because of this adaptation, as well as the easy climate, many other hardwood trees and shrubs can be evergreen, such as Mexican elder, manzanita, dwarf coniferous pines, mountain mahogany, sugar sumac, bitter cherry, California fremontia, sagebrush, coyote brush, chamiso, and yucca.

There is a tremendous variety of habitats within this region, forming a patchwork landscape of forests, woodlands, savannas, scrub, and grasslands. Differing habitats are woven together in complex patterns created by variations in soil, landscape, wind, sun, and fire histories.

In the spring, when the soil holds the largest amount of water, this area is a patchwork of bright-colored blossoms. Later, when temperatures heat up and the water in the soil evaporates, wind-scattered seeds begin to mature, but will remain dormant in the earth until the rains begin. Evergreen shrubs are more tolerant of drought, and begin to grow when the seasonal rains have passed and water has found its way deep into the ground.

The summer climate makes the region prone to fires caused naturally by lightning. The California Indians often used fire to clear brush and trees, in order to make way for grasses and other vegetation that would support game animals and useful crops. As a result, the fire-loving plants became more common, while others less so. After European colonization, regular burning was discontinued, so fuel began to build up. Now, when fires do occur, they are much more destructive.

Mediterranean regions all over the world are some of the most favorable for human habitation. In the Southern Pacific coastal region, people have had a great impact on the native plant and animal species of the area through extensive agriculture and overgrazing, logging, disruption of the natural fire regime, and use of large tracts of land for the building of homes and cities. People immigrating to this pleasant region have also brought in many exotic plants and animals that crowd out indigenous species.

The California chaparral contains many diverse animals. Some common predators are mountain lion, bobcat and coyote, as well as many Red-tailed Hawks, Sharp-shinned Hawks, and the Golden Eagle. Other birds also make the chaparral their home, including quail, roadrunners and Scrub Jays, as well as many species of reptiles, rodents and insects.

Sadly, many indigenous species of plant and animal are in danger of extinction, due to habitat loss, predation or disease brought in by non-native species. To say a plant or animal is exotic is perhaps confusing, as even cats and dogs, or species of wildflowers, if they have not originated in a specific region, may be considered exotic. They could be native to another part of North America, but with no natural enemies in the area, they can out-compete species naturally evolved to be part of the ecosystem.[2]

Riparian woodlands can be found in ribbon-like bands along streams where rich soils and high humidity produce a natural greenhouse effect. Although this unique community accounts for less than one per cent of California's total forest acreage, it supports one of the most diverse ecological communities of plants and animals in the region. Tall deciduous trees, such as western sycamore, and the evergreen California bay laurel tower above a lush understory of ferns and delicate wildflowers.[3]

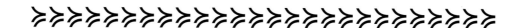

‹ Southern Pacific Coast : Mediterranean Chaparral and Riparian Woodlands ›

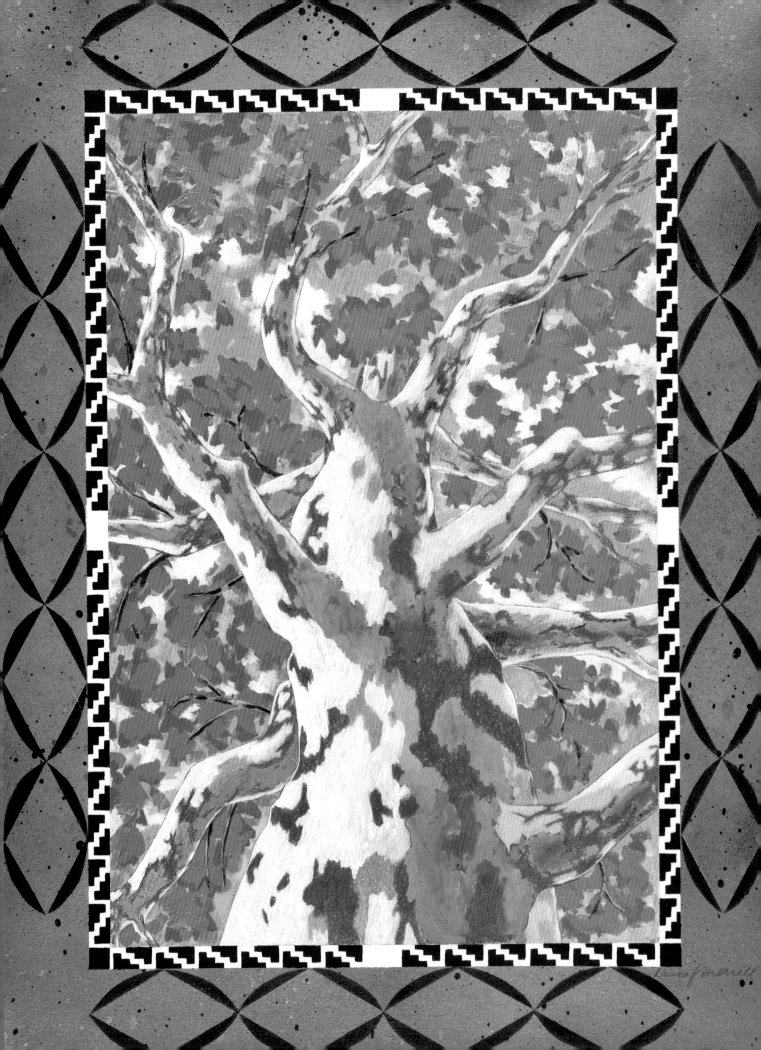

REFLECTIONS ON PEACE

What Sycamore Can You About Itself

*P*eace is a *flowing* quality, in which I feel that I am gently moving forward, without care for the future, watching the movements of all things—the animals and the plants, as well as the stars and planets. Peace manifests when a summer thunderstorm slowly gathers shape on the horizon, when the air is still before dawn, or when something dies and its inner form moves away.

When I dream, I imagine flying up into the stratosphere, to observe the whole Earth at once. I see the movement of the clouds and the patterns they form, and love the swirling, interlacing spirals. It appears as if they are going somewhere exceedingly important, tumbling over each other in friendly rivalry. From here, I see that *everything* simply moves past and around me, like time and the air.

I enjoy being near a constant source of water, to feel the damp greenness of the wind off the ocean, and to experience the warm rays of the morning sun on my body.

I am one of the "Old Ones." At the time my species was young, the colors of the sky were extraordinary—there was much more red. Sometimes I recall things about the ancient times—lumbering dinosaurs, and others who have become extinct. In past lives, I have been a cloud, a bit of the sky, or sea foam.

Sycamore's Place in the World

Sycamore is a link between the distant—far distant—past, and the present. Since the advent of mankind and human civilization, Sycamore has become a reminder that although *homo sapiens* is the dominant species now, they are not alone, and need the companionship of all other forms of life.

The Sycamore is part of a family that emerges from the Source that dwells at the center of time. This family understands that our planet spins, but the spinning is measured, forming a stable, but barely perceptible background sensation of security.

This particular member of the family, California Sycamore, is a still presence within the center of our busy days, around which all things can circulate and have their own important moment, as do the spokes of a wheel.

Sycamore's Message for Us

Understanding my concept of Peace could give you the ability to weather emotional storms without *your* roots being ripped from the soil. Embracing an eyes-wide-open form of meditation provides stability and focus. It would also instill an awareness of being separate, but connected, not only to your own kind, but to the surroundings as well.

I see that Peace manifests in you already, in your recognition that "life goes on" after traumatic events, without being dismissive of the worth or significance of others who have moved on from of your immediate sphere of experience.

The contribution of your species to the planet is the ability to bring a sense of ownership going beyond your own species. Your task is to broaden that sense ever further. It is not sufficient to be simply "cutters of the grass"—those who take without returning something of value to the mix.

Your seed will carry you into the future. Be adaptable, patient, and persevering.

Reach for altruism in your sense of ownership and responsibility. Make your goal to be more caring, less pragmatic. Care less about the "usefulness" of something in relation to your own "future generations." Realize that the future generations of humanity depend on *fully* comprehending that "We are all one."

As we move through time, our intention, our reaching and longing give us passage through space. Desire is pure intention. Out of our desire, the Future will manifest. Our Fate is inextricably linked to our Desire. Death is simply a different kind of passage, and a chance to begin again.

Be brave in your approach to living, but enjoy what you are, like the opossum hanging by his tail.

Don't settle for "just survival." Be a cacophony of color.

< 48 >

< Secret Voices from the Forest >

CHRONICLES

Sycamores, also called plane trees, are among the most common shade and ornamental trees planted in North America and Europe. The sycamore of the Bible is actually a fig, noted for its use by ancient Egyptians to make mummy cases. The potential life span of a California sycamore can be five hundred to six hundred years, and it can reach eighty to one hundred feet in height. It grows slowly and can have a massive, barrel-shaped trunk that leans and forks into picturesque shapes, often resting on the ground. The current champion was measured in 1998, in San Juan, Capistrano. It was, at that time, 95 feet tall and 117 feet in diameter, with a 108-foot crown spread.[4]

Sycamores are members of one of the planet's oldest family of trees, thought to be over one hundred million years old. Fossil leaves, fruit heads, and pollen grains of this family, amazingly similar to living plane trees, have been preserved in sedimentary rocks around the Northern Hemisphere. These fossils demonstrate that the forests covering North America

‹ Southern Pacific Coast : Mediterranean Chaparral and Riparian Woodlands : California Sycamore ›

were once continuous, both to Asia in the West, and to Europe in the East. North American species have been geographically isolated from those in Eurasia for tens of millions of years, but the North American species are still capable of producing fertile hybrids when crossed with Eurasian species.

Native from southeastern Europe to India, the Oriental plane reaches one hundred feet. Its bristly seed balls hang in clusters of two to six. The London plane is a hybrid between the American and the Oriental planes, combining characteristics of both in varying degrees, and is planted widely in cities for its resistance to air pollution and to diseases that more readily affect other plane trees. It is a little shorter and squatter than the American tree and usually has bristly, paired seed balls. The California sycamore has contorted branches, thick leaves, and bristly seed balls in groups of two to seven.

< 50 >

The American plane tree—the sycamore common to the eastern half of North America—is the tallest of the plane tree species, sometimes reaching a height of more than 160 feet. Its smooth, ball-shaped seed clusters usually dangle singly, and often persist after the leaves of the tree fall. All planes grow rapidly and furnish quick shade.

The California sycamore has distinctive, mottled bark, speckled shades of tan, white, grey, green, and sometimes yellow. The rigid texture of the bark tissue lacks the power to expand with growth, so the older, darker bark peels away to accommodate new wood growth.

It has been noticed that there is little underbrush beneath sycamores in the wild, so the bark is often used for mulch, as it has allelopathic qualities, meaning that this species can suppress the growth of another species by the release of toxic substances.

A deciduous tree pollinated by wind, it has unisexual flower heads produced in conspicuous, ball-like clusters, with tiny flowers densely packed around a solid core. These clusters are attached to pendulous stalks that hang below the leaves. Separate male and female flowers are produced on the same plant.

The Western sycamore prefers to have its roots near water, and they can develop to a depth of at least seven meters. Although it doesn't tolerate long periods of flooding, the sycamore can survive extended droughts.

California Indian tribes used the sycamore's limbs to build their houses, and made decoctions from the bark to be used for asthma or as a tonic for the blood. For these remedies, the bark was cleaned and boiled till the water turned red, after which it could be drunk hot or cold.

Many Species of birds, such as the Red-tailed Hawk, Anna's Hummingbird, Cedar

< Secret Voices from the Forest >

Waxwing, and Acorn Woodpecker depend upon trees such as the sycamore for habitat and nesting, because of their large canopies. Heron and egret rookeries are often found in stands of sycamores, and some birds will nest in the peeling bark. Western sycamore snags are especially important to cavity-nesters in mixed riparian forests, such as Barn Owls and ringtail cats, which all nest in sycamore cavities.

A large sycamore tree played a role in the establishment of the city of Los Angeles. The native Gabrielino or Tongva people had a village called Yangna, at that time located near a huge California sycamore tree, under which they held meetings. The Spanish settlement that later gave way to the pueblo of Los Angeles was located next to Yangna, in sight of this sycamore tree. Although the settlement was destroyed in 1815 in a large flood, the tree survived. Later it was found that the tree was over four hundred years old.[5]

< 51 >

Sycamore seeds went along with Astronaut Stuart Roosa in the lunar orbit of Apollo 14 in 1971, as part of a joint N.A.S.A./U.S.F.S. project to see if close proximity to the moon would affect their growth.

After being chosen for the mission, Roosa was contacted by the U.S. Forest Service, who knew him from his days as a smoke jumper. The Apollo astronauts were permitted to take a few small personal items along with them into space. Stuart Roosa wanted to honor the U.S.F.S., so agreed to take hundreds of tree seeds with him on the mission, packed in his personal kit in small containers.

Five different types of seeds were chosen: Loblolly pine, sycamore, sweetgum, redwood, and Douglas fir. After their return, the seeds were germinated and planted by the Forest Service. Known as the "Moon Trees," the resulting seedlings were distributed throughout the United States, many as part of the nation's bicentennial celebration in 1976. One was planted at the White House, and many universities and colleges received seedlings, but as the selected tree species were from the southern and western U.S., not all states were given one of the Moon Trees. Some were even sent to other parts of the world, such as the one presented to the Emperor of Japan. Official record was never kept of the locations of all the plantings. At present, members of N.A.S.A. are enlisting the public's help in finding the sites of the plantings, and in ascertaining if they are still standing. More information, and a list of Moon Tree locations can be found at several websites.[6]

< Southern Pacific Coast : Mediterranean Chaparral and Riparian Woodlands : California Sycamore >

CALIFORNIA SYCAMORE COMPANIONS

White-Throated Swift
Hollyleaf Cherry
California Torreya
Western Spadefoot Toad

California Condor
Desert Bell
Arboreal Salamander
Orangebush Monkeyflower
Rustic Sphinx Moth

Sea Otter
Common Madia
Bitter Dogbane
Jerusalem Cricket

Chaparral Pea
California Gnatcatcher
Parry's Larkspur
Narrow-faced Kangaroo Rat
Trametes Versicolor

Planted like tall, big-boned

mothers-on-patrol where streets

and thoroughfares break

from the ground and grow and branch

and suffer seasons of decay,

then rise again, their symbiotic builders

succeeding each other in a blur

of generations, generations

with machines, rapid and careless,

obeying their own blind natures,

we clean and calm their noisy air,

shade them from the glare of the sun,

lend them our leaves,

    because all things

        obey their own natures,

            wherein they are free.

FACTS ABOUT SOME SYCAMORE COMPANIONS

California Condor

The scientific name, *Gymnogyps californianus*, comes from the Greek word *gymnast*, meaning naked, and refers to the head; *gyps* is Greek for "a vulture;" and the Latinized word for California indicates the bird's range. The name "condor" is from the Spanish word *cuntur*, and is the Incan name given to the Andean Condor.

California Condors, the largest flying birds in North America, are monogamous and pair for life. They only become adults after six or seven years, and can live up to sixty years in the wild—much longer than most other kinds of birds.

Ten thousand years ago, California Condors roamed the entirety of both coasts of North America. By about 1900, the condor population had decreased dramatically. It was eventually limited to southern California, because of loss of habitat, low birth rate, poisoning, and shooting.

In the 1970s, it was found that only a few dozen condors remained in the wild. In 1980, a conservation project was begun, in an attempt to save the birds from extinction. Some birds were fitted with radio transmitters. Wild eggs were collected and hatched at the Los Angeles Zoo and San Diego Wild Animal Park, helping to increase the population. A few birds were taken to the zoos for captive breeding. But it was too late to stop the decline in the wild bird population, so in the mid-1980s, all of the remaining condors in the wild were captured and taken to zoos.

The last wild condor was captured in 1987. The entire world population of the species, at that time, was twenty-seven birds, and all were housed in two captive-breeding facilities in southern California. These individuals were Topatopa, the first, captured in 1967, nine once-free-flying adult and immature birds trapped from 1982 to 1987, four young birds removed as nestlings from nests from 1982 to 1984, and thirteen captive-reared condors hatched from eggs removed from nests in 1983 through 1986.

Today, their numbers have increased to more than 160 birds living in the wild. Designated refuges and captive breeding programs are helping to protect and restore the species.

They can be found in or near Grand Canyon National Park, Glen Canyon National Recreation Area, Pinnacles National Monument, and Big Sur.[7]

< Secret Voices from the Forest >

< 54 >

California Torreya

Many trees have lost a large part of their original prehistoric range because of climate change. The California torreya is one of two remaining types in North America. The other is in Florida, where Connie Barlow, the web spokesperson for the Torreya Guardians, is making an effort to keep that variety from extinction.

She theorizes that the endangered eastern member of the yew family migrated to the Florida area during the last ice age, and was stranded after the ice flows receded. She proposes the Florida torreya be "rewilded" to the mountainous areas further north, to secure its survival as a species.[8]

Sea Otter

The sea otter is a member of the weasel family, spending most of its time in the water, even to sleep. Sea Otters are very social animals, and may congregate in large groups—the males in one group, and the females and pups in another. They often anchor themselves in kelp forests to keep from drifting in the currents.

< 55 >

Their nostrils and ears close in the water, and they have webbed feet and water-repellent fur. Their fur is in two layers, one trapping a layer of air next to their skin. Theirs is the thickest fur of any mammal, at nearly a million hairs per square inch.

They hunt and eat in the water. They are one of the few animals to use tools—placing a rock on their stomachs as they float, and smashing a clam or crab against the rock to break it open.

The sea otter also gives birth in the water, and the mother holds its pup on her chest when she nurses. When it is first born, the mother wraps the pup in kelp when leaving to hunt. The baby's fur traps so much air it floats easily on top of the water. After about four weeks, the pup is ready to begin swimming on its own, but stays with its mother for the first eight months.

< Southern Pacific Coast : Mediterranean Chaparral and Riparian Woodlands : California Sycamore >

The Orangebush Monkeyflower

This flowering plant of the southwestern coast of North America has sticky, dark green leaves and occurs in a variety of shades, from white to red, although light orange is the most common color. The Miwok and Pomo Indians used it as an antiseptic, as it sped the healing of minor scrapes and burns.

Monkeyflowers are honey plants, and are attractive to bees and hummingbirds. As such, they are a useful component of a habitat garden, or wildlife garden—a deliberately created environment that attracts various kinds of wildlife, such as birds, amphibians, reptiles, insects, and mammals.

A wildlife garden will usually contain habitats that are as much as possible like those that would have been native before urbanization. A habitat garden can contain nest boxes for birds, bees, and even insects, log piles, which provide shelter for lizards and worms, ponds, which will draw birds, butterflies, frogs, toads, and plants and wildflowers to attract beneficial insects.

This kind of gardening always aims at using only the most frugal application of supplemental water, and the plants used are primarily native to the area. The focus is to aim for symbiotic, and thereby self-sustaining relationships between plants and animals. The National Wildlife Federation and others give tips on creating habitat gardens.[9]

White-throated Swift

A highly social creature, the White-throated Swift sleeps in roosts with hundreds of other swifts, typically in larger cavities in cliffs and large rocks. In the evening they gather above a roost, ascending beyond view, and then descend as a group.

With a swirling in front of the roost crack, individuals enter the roost several abreast. Occasionally one misses, bouncing off the entrance to rejoin the swirling masses.

White-throated Swifts are among the most accomplished fliers of all North American birds. They streak forward at high speed, suddenly changing direction with lightning-fast adjustments of wing and tail. The generic name of this species is particularly apt: *Aeronautess*, or "Sky Sailor."[10]

Trametes Versicolor

Also called "Turkey Tails," this is a mushroom that has been used for centuries in Chinese medicine as a tonic. There is quite a bit of research being done to investigate its possible use as a treatment for various sorts of cancer.[11]

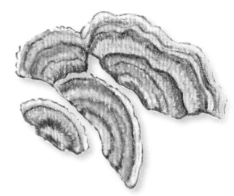

Western Spadefoot Toad

Spadefoot toads are so named for a sharp-edged keratinous outgrowth on each hind foot. This feature enables them to burrow vertically into sandy or loose soils. Spadefoots are generally found in arid climates, where they spend most of their time buried in the ground, but later emerge during heavy rains to breed and lay eggs.

Amphibians are older than the dinosaurs. In fact, they were the first group of vertebrates to set out on land some 350 million years ago. All other terrestrial vertebrates, from dinosaurs to humans, owe their existence to the amphibians.

Amphibians are an important, but often overlooked part of the environment. An individual toad eats thousands of insects over one summer, and in turn, many fish and birds eat amphibian eggs and larvae. Since amphibians are sensitive to changes in both water quality and adjacent land-use practices, their populations can serve as indicators of overall environmental quality.

Jerusalem Cricket

This is a relatively large, rather bizarre-looking, but inoffensive insect that can be seen frequently in Mexico, along the Pacific coast, and throughout the western United States. It is also referred to as the potato bug, "the old bald man," and in Spanish, *el niño de la tierra* — the child of the earth.

One amusing account of how it acquired its name is that at the time the European settlers first came to the west, a slang term to express surprise was, "Jerusalem!"

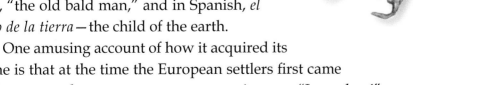

REFLECTIONS on GRACE

What Elder Can Tell You About Itself

*G*race signifies abundance. What is required is always in evidence. Always. Blooming and fruiting are spontaneous emergences from within, as an expression of *becoming*. They arise upon, and are held up by, a cushion of *be*longing.

Grace manifests in moments of beauty, which dissolve an instant later: in a bird singing, when the rains come and the river flows, in the uncertain certainty of a sunrise.

In my dreams I feel myself tumbling—the physical sensation that accompanies growing. My leaves and branches meander and rotate, going in all directions—sometimes up into the sky, sometimes down into the earth.

Life and Death are two aspects of movement, action and non-action. It all begins with anticipation, when I am aroused in spring by Desire. I respond to the ebb and flow of the seasons—first with leaves, flowers, youth and attraction, then with ripeness, berries, fruition and fulfillment. Life turns; the seasons turn. When apprehension fills me, I can tell the future.

Nevertheless, I am content to hear the dolphins play. It is enough to become a place for the birds to rest while they turn silence into joy.

Elder's Place in the World

Mexican Elder shows that we can live in the moment if we will learn to mimic the immediacy of seasonal change. Elder's own transformations emulate the motion of Time, never ceasing. The sleep of Death lasts only a short space, till Desire wakes us again in the spring.

What is known to exist in the mind of Spirit comes into being when flowers bloom like a bridal bouquet and succulent berries ripen like kisses. This is the Future made manifest.

Elder makes full use of the time and place in which it finds itself. In so doing, it has become a bright presence that brings pleasure and security to others. This can tell us that we have a choice of responses to what appears to be our fate. With acceptance and contentment, further possibilities may come more easily within reach. Through understanding that our needs will always be fulfilled, the selfishness that comes from fear—a sense that you need to protect what is "yours"—will dissolve.

Elder is part of the Honeysuckle Family, a group of shrubs and trees that produce small fruits eaten by a host of birds and small animals. This family specializes in being sweet and inviting, which urges all who come for sustenance to also partake of the products of the soul.

The Mexican Elder has particular charm, and uses its scent, color, pollen and fruit to draw in the beasts of the air and the field.

This family has learned that although the resources of the Earth are indeed bountiful, these endless gifts may not be so, as the time in which we live is changeable.

Elder's Message for Us

Call to the wind. It will answer you.

Grace manifests in you through the act of sharing your bounty with those who are convinced they have less, be they human, animal or plant.

You have an innate knowledge of cooperative effort—but one that goes beyond that of the hive or herd. It allows for revelation to be your directional force. Humanity's contribution to the world will be the *result* of not accepting its apparent fate. Do not let insecurity or fear of change suppress those who are able to inspire and manifest exceptional leadership qualities. Otherwise you are going backwards, which will only bring you suffering.

Do not be afraid to tap into the Source on your own. But if you would act like a butterfly, then like the Monarch, it would be good for you to be part of a large group. While it is not necessary or practical for all to be leaders, those who blindly follow create dead weight, which must then be carried by the rest.

Take time to dream about the sap running through your body. Its source is that which animates *all* life—and yet, we all appear to be different. Learn to recognize the true nature of divergence, and the conditions by which it emerges. Your task is to become authentic.

One of the characteristics of Spirit is the convergence of energy. Embrace this quality, and there will be no such thing as a problem.

Believe in Practical Magic.

CHRONICLES

The Mexican elder, or desert elderberry, is the largest elder in North America. It is also the southernmost, and because of this, is mostly evergreen. It blooms and fruits all year long, and has been an important food source for both wildlife and American Indian tribes.

Using the leaves, flowers and berries of this tree for food and medicine, wood, tools, weapons, and dye, the California Indian tribes found the Mexican elder an important resource.

They called it the "tree of music," because they used hollowed-out stems to make flutes. With four to six holes, the pre-contact aboriginal flute is tuned to ancient musical scales, which even the best flute players of today find difficult to play without the addition of a mouthpiece.

The Riverside Municipal Museum has examples of these rare instruments, and some modern musicians have created replicas of the original elderberry cane flutes played by the Kumeyaay-Diegueño Indians of Southern California.[12]

The California Indians also used Mexican elder to make a percussion instrument called the "clapperstick," which was sounded when the split end was slapped on the palm of the hand, or shaken to make a quick rattling sound. It was used instead of a drum, to keep the rhythm of the song or dance.

However, the widest use of elderberries is for cooking, baking, and making jams and wine. It may remind us of Cary Grant's old aunties, in the movie Arsenic and Old Lace, who

‹ Southern Pacific Coast : Mediterranean Chaparral and Riparian Woodlands : Mexican Elder ›

served a delightful elderberry wine (laced with arsenic) to their ill-fated "gentlemen."

Making wine at home was once a common practice, as was making jams and jellies and preserving the produce from the home garden. With a growing interest in home, rooftop, and small-space gardens, these activities are enjoying a revival.

In the April/May 2009 issue of *Winemaker* magazine, author and avid winemaker, Jack Keller, describes making elderberry wine in great detail, all the way from growing and harvesting the berries to cleaning the kitchen utensils. He also gives advice, book reviews, historical information and recipes on his own website, including recipes for watermelon and dandelion wines.[13]

It is important to remember never to eat wild elderberries raw, as they contain a toxin called hydrocyanic acid. Cooking will destroy it in most species of elderberry; the exception is the red elderberry species, which should never be eaten at all.

In a 1995 Israeli study, elderberry extract was found to reduce both the severity of symptoms and the duration of the flu (two to three days in the treated group versus six days in the placebo group), using an extract standardized to contain 5 percent total flavonoids, in a 500 milligram dose, twice daily.[14]

A fairly standard recipe for elderberry syrup is: equal amounts of elderberry juice (obtained by heating crushed berries at a very low temperature until the juice releases, then straining out the pulp and seeds) and sweetening agent, either honey or sugar, and the addition of something to preserve it, such as lemon juice or 80 proof vodka. The resulting syrup can be used to treat colds and flu, or taken by the morning tablespoon as a preventative tonic.

As well as its use for medicinal teas and salves, elder flowers and berries are made into fritters and muffins. One can also brew a love charm made from the plant's five-petal flowers, as the number five has long been held sacred to the Goddess.

Varieties of sambuccus have had some interesting traditional uses. The strong-smelling foliage was once tied to a horse's mane, to keep flies away while riding. The pith of the elder tree is very light, and was used by watchmakers as an abrasive for cleaning tools before intricate work.

< 62 >

< Secret Voices from the Forest >

There is extensive folklore associating the elder with witches. Some legends say the tree wards off evil influence and gives protection, and villagers planted elder near the doors of their cottages for that reason.

Other beliefs claim that witches considered the plant sacred, and would not use it for common purposes, such as bonfires. A reference to the sacred relationship of the elder to witches appears in Harry Potter and the Deathly Hallows, by J.K. Rowling, in which "the most powerful wand" is made of elder.

The elderberry has a long cultural history of folktales and myth in its European incarnation, Sambuccus nigra. According to pagan legend, the tree was inhabited by a wood nymph called the "Elder Mother." If given due respect, she was benevolent with her protection and medicinal gifts. However, she could be vindictive if a careless wood-cutter dared to construct his home or household furniture from the wood of the tree without permission. The tree spirit would attack, causing mysterious accidents to befall the hapless homeowner.[15]

The requirement of preserving food for use through the cold dark of winter has been integral to human survival for as long as our species has lived in organized societies. Many rituals of thanks and entreaty have sprung from the activities surrounding these necessary tasks, varying according to whether the food was gathered from the wild, or a product of agriculture or animal husbandry.

Harvest Festivals are common to all cultures, bringing us closer together in community, and begin with the "first fruits" of the season. First fruits are a religious offering of the first agricultural produce of the harvest. In Classical Greece, the first fruits were offered as a sacrifice in the temples of the Eleusinian goddesses, Demeter and her daughter, Persephone. Much of the produce was sold to pay for the upkeep of the temples.

Similarly, the Celtic holiday of Lughnassadh, or Lammas, also called "The Feast of First Fruits," begins the harvest season. It is equivalent to the Pilgrim's thanksgiving, for if crops were planted on time in spring, the harvest would begin in late summer rather than fall. Lammas is primarily an agricultural event. For farmers and herdsmen in an agricultural society, it was a thanksgiving ritual to ensure a good harvest, and thus a prosperous winter.

‹ Southern Pacific Coast : Mediterranean Chaparral and Riparian Woodlands : Mexican Elder ›

MEXICAN ELDER COMPANIONS

California Leaf-nosed Bat
Powdery Dudleya
California Maidenhair Fern
Long-beaked Dolphin

Common Side-blotched Lizard
Snowplant
Banded Alder Borer
Elegant Brodiaea
Green-tailed Towhee

West Coast Lady
Geastrum Floriforme
Red Maids
Red-eared Slider

California Washingtonia Palm
Cinnamon Teal
Wild Orange Poppy
California Dogface
McNab Cypress

Here they come
in grave procession, arms raised,
wrists supple, dancing
on warm airs, green sleeved, hands
flourishing garlands of flowers,
clotted and rich,
pouring like still cream,
bending with bowls of living lace,
one after another,
stepping gently with breezes,
balancing about them
intricate clusters of fruit
the color of jewels—aventurine,
clouded opal, fiery garnet—
from delicate fingers let loose,
tipped out on the earth,
piled on the great earth
till rivers run with them,
till mountains groan with them;
    O here they come
        in grave procession,
            bringing the gifts of time.

FACTS ABOUT SOME MEXICAN ELDER COMPANIONS

California Leaf-nosed Bat

This is the only North American bat north of Mexico that has large ears and leaf-like projections on the nose. It is also one of the most able to maneuver in flight. With short, broad wings, it can fly at low speeds using minimal energy.

The average lifespan of a leaf-nosed bat is twenty to thirty years in the wild. This species cannot crawl on its thumbs and toes like most bats, but has excellent night vision and hearing. It can see insects by starlight and hear a cricket's footsteps.[16]

< 66 >

Snow Plant

This is the most colorful example of a strange group of parasitic plants that lives on fungi, which are other parasites! Botanists call them "mycotrophic wildflowers," which means "fungus nutrition."

The snow plant is the unlikely relation of such shrubs as manzanita, madrone, laurel, and azalea. The scientific name, *Sarcodes sanguinea Torrye*, translates roughly to "the bloody flesh-like thing," an allusion to the bright red color of the plant.[17]

Side-blotched Lizard

The most abundant and commonly seen lizard in the deserts and semi-arid areas, the side-blotched lizard is active only during the day. Due to its small size, it warms quickly, and is usually the first lizard species to emerge in the morning. It is inactive during cold weather.

Its tail is often broken off when a lizard is captured, but will grow back with time. At an average of about one year, this lizard's life span is short.

< Secret Voices from the Forest >

Biologist Barry Sinervo from the University of California, Santa Cruz, who has been studying the behavior of *Uta stansburiana* since 1989, discovered an interesting evolutionary strategy in the mating behavior of this lizard species.

Males have various throat colorations—orange, blue or yellow. Each type follows a fixed, heritable mating strategy.

Orange-throated males, who are strongest and do not form strong pair bonds, usurp territory.

Blue-throated males are middle-sized, forming strong pair bonds with their mates. Individually, they are out-competed by orange-throated males, but by locating near other, unrelated blue males, cooperating to guard mates and defend territory, they become more successful.

Yellow-throated males are the smallest of the three, and cannot win in direct confrontation, but their coloration mimics that of females. Under this disguise, they sneak behind the backs of the blue-throats and mate with their females while they are engaged in fights with the orange-throats.

Summarized as "orange beats blue, blue beats yellow, and yellow beats orange," Sinervo has described this behavior as being similar to the rules of rock-paper-scissors. These strategies appear to result in an evolutionarily stable situation in which no color morph can dominate the population.[18]

< 67 >

Powdery Dudleya

The powdery dudleya is a succulent, or "fat plant." Succulents naturally retain water and are adapted to arid climates or unfavorable soil conditions.

This plant is one of several species that can be found along the pacific coast of North America. It often forms a large mat, and can vary greatly in appearance. Although not lacking in moisture, the typical climate near the seacoast exposes plants to high levels of dissolved minerals that are deadly to many plant species.

With a waxy outer surface that creates a humid microhabitat around the plant, surface air movement is reduced, creating shade and reducing water loss.[19]

< Southern Pacific Coast : Mediterranean Chaparral and Riparian Woodlands : Mexican Elder >

Red-eared Slider

These turtles love to bask. They are seen in large numbers on logs or other available spots out of the water, but seldom on the bank. It is not unusual to see them basking in piles three and four deep if individual spots are scarce.

They can apprehend the approach of a predator or potential danger through their extraordinary sensitivity to feel vibrations, and will quickly retreat to the water if they feel threatened. Turtles have a fully developed inner ear structure, but no external opening. Red-eared turtles spend a considerable amount of time just floating, using their inflated throat as a flotation device.

Male red-ears mature in two to five years. Adult males have long front toenails that are used in courtship. When the male chooses his partner, he will swim in front of her, stretch out his forelimbs with palms turned out so as to just touch the sides of the lady's head, and vibrate his nails against her face. This courtship dance is often seen during the warmer months.[20]

< 68 >

California Washingtonia Palm

There are 2,500 species of palms worldwide, with eleven native to North America. The largest of these, and the only palm tree native to western North America, is the California Washingtonia. It is also known as the desert palm and the California fan palm.

Fan-shaped leaves spread from around the top of the tree, while numerous old, dead leaves hang down against the trunk. The dead leaves form a protective area that provides a home and gives shelter to many birds, insects and small rodents.

Groves of the rare fan palm can be seen in Anza-Borrego Desert State Park, near Palm Springs, California, in Joshua Tree National Park, and near Yuma, Arizona.

The original California fan palm oases were important gathering and habitation sites for native tribes, and were indicative of important springs—usually located along earthquake faults. Some of these included Thousand Palms, Palm Canyon and Andreas Canyon.

< Secret Voices from the Forest >

California Dog-faced Butterfly

In the 1920s, members of the Lorquin Entomological Society of Los Angeles began a search to find an official state butterfly for California. The final three candidates were: the Lorquin's admiral, the California sister and the California dogface.

After heated debates, it was agreed that the California dogface should be the state butterfly. The primary circumstance that affected the decision was the fact that the California dogface was the only one of the three butterflies that finds its home *only* in California.[21]

Earthstar

Tiny at 5 centimeters or less, the *Geastrum floriforme* is a species of fungus related to puff balls. The name comes from *geo* meaning "earth" and *aster* meaning "star." Initially a perfect sphere, the thick outer casing splits into star-shaped sections whose tips touch the ground, elevating the spore sac. When rain touches the inner sphere, the spores puff out into the air.

Green-tailed Towhee

Pipilo chlorurus is a member of the sparrow family. It is fairly common in habitats with sagebrush and other shrubs, as its tendency is to stay under cover.

A group of towhees is collectively known as a "tangle" or a "teapot" of towhees. (Who decides these things?) The scientific name means, approximately, "colorful chirper."[22]

⪻ CALIFORNIA BAY LAUREL ⪼

REFLECTIONS ON FREEDOM

What Laurel Can Tell You About Itself

*F*reedom signifies movement and change. For me, this means many trunks going in all directions, as well as the spaces between. When a *place* is made for the space between, the Invisible Ones have more room to bounce around. They are energy "thoughts" that spend the days investigating, and are a microcosm of the essential nature of Spirit in that respect. The Invisible Ones are not invisible to everyone, so those that can see them make way. It's a courtesy not often shown.

When I dream, I visit a place that is the source of timelessness and strength, where even the color of the air is more vibrant. In this place, I also have the ability to see in all directions at once. It is a skill that I bring back with me when I return to the here and now. You might think that all trees would have that ability, because of our Earthly form, but you would be wrong. The self-awareness of some other kinds of trees extends from a particular leaf, stem, branch, trunk, or root at any given moment. It is directional, and primarily has to do with movement . . . or so I have been told.

Freedom, which exemplifies change, manifests everywhere and in everything—eternally. Likewise, all things move constantly, although some do so more rapidly than others. In truth, objects that appear to move slowly are vibrating at so quickly you cannot see it happening, like rocks and mountains, which give the illusion that they are not moving at all!

Freedom can also be observed in the way a cloud can travel where it wishes, or appear and disappear at will. This is energy that moves quickly, morphing in and out of existence, but like the boulders and mountains, will become more solid during a storm.

Laurel's Place in the World

The California Bay Laurel belongs to a large family of tropical species. Like many of those who dwell in the tropics, it has a taste for melodrama and song. Men who knew the Laurel long ago thought there was a God-like spirit contained there, and that the tree was the vehicle for qualities not normally having solid form. As an aspect of Spirit, these qualities were assigned intent and personality, and sometimes a human shape. This allowed men to attribute their own mysterious actions and feelings to something outside of themselves.

The West Wind is Laurel's friend, as it whistles a tune that inspires curiosity, and an interest in going forward into the future. Another aspect of Laurel's place in this world is to be a connector of water with air. This is one reason why it is attracted to clouds.

Laurel's spirit moves in a spiral, pushing its way into the Earth. The movement of this vortex reflects a relationship to the currents of the winds, which also move in interlocking spirals. These spirals proceed towards the future as a manifestation of Time, very much like a "black hole." This species of Laurel has learned, through pushing its way into the earth, that the warmth of the Earth's core is what causes the nurturing warmth in the surrounding atmosphere.

Laurel teaches us about the paradox of Freedom in this way: in order to be completely whole and independent, we must allow for the definition of "I" to be blurred by the influence of others. In truth, we cross over the insubstantial borders of self all the time. However, it is not necessary to defend one's own space, as each individual atom is needed in order for a larger entity to become manifest.

Laurel's Message for Us

In you, freedom appears as changeability in the fluidity of emotions. Now you feel one thing, and a little later, the exact opposite. And yet, both are "true" and completely justifiable by the "facts." This may seem fickle and inconstant, but on the other hand, it gives you the capacity to "stand in another's shoes."

You are constantly looking for solutions. This would seem to indicate that you feel that nothing is quite adequate the way it is at the moment, but this drive is a manifestation of the essence of life, which is always changing, always moving towards a state of equilibrium.

This urge is omnipresent, but comes from the unconscious. Through your unique ability to observe yourselves, you will bring the desire for solutions further into the realm of consciousness, making choices geared towards constructive change. It is difficult to see the end result of this process. The unconscious is powerful, but because it cannot be directly seen, there may be no possibility to alter its intent.

Create a vortex. It will channel energy down into the earth. A tornado, although it can be destructive, is like lightning, creating a channel that directs spirit into the heart of the planet.

Freedom also comes to those who follow the wind with their senses. It is like a dream of being a cloud, being blown about, as if one had no physical body.

The sea level has risen and fallen more than once. Do not fear change. Worry will only serve to nullify the effects that are *possible* for you to create.

Try to identify less with your physical manifestation. This is an experience that coincides with your perception of time and the alteration of the physical body. It appears to be born, mature, age and die. If you wish to be free of the stress this attachment causes you, allow your perception to open up like a flower. It is a joyful adventure simply to exist.

CHRONICLES

< 73 >

The California bay laurel occupies moist canyons and valleys, all along the California coast and into Oregon. It is one of two New World members of the tropical Laurel family. The other is sassafras, a tree of the eastern part of North America.

This is a familiar tree of the forests of California. It is unmistakable, due to the powerful scent of its leaves. When rubbed or crushed, the leaves emit an odor reminiscent of the bay leaf of the Mediterranean, but typically the California laurel has a much stronger scent. This odor is due to the large percentage of aromatic oils present in the leaves.

Like its relative, the European bay laurel, its leaves can be used for cooking, but since they are so much more pungent, they should be used sparingly. When crushed, they release a sharp, camphor-like volatile oil. It is said that putting a piece of the leaf in your hatband can cure a headache, but also cause one.

< Southern Pacific Coast : Mediterranean Chaparral and Riparian Woodlands : Bay Laurel >

The California Indians placed laurel boughs on a fire, and then breathed in the smoke to clear their nasal passages. Boughs were also hung in houses to repel fleas and mice. One popular use for the leaves that has persisted is to put them in between bed mattresses to prevent, or get rid of, flea infestations.

The leaves were also gathered and used to ward off evil spirits, bad luck, rheumatism and insects. They were burned as a prayer or offering when calling in good spirits and spiritual protection, to promote healing, or when requesting luck for gambling.

The Chilula Indians believed the tree to have special power—the nuts were eaten prior to a hunting trip for good luck, before going into a war battle, or as a cure for internal sickness. Roasted, shelled "bay nuts" were eaten whole, or ground into powder and prepared as a drink resembling unsweetened chocolate. The flavor, depending on the darkness of the roast, has been described variously as "roast coffee," "dark chocolate," or "burnt popcorn."

The inner nut is purported to contain powerful stimulants similar to caffeine, although this information is known only through anecdotal reports. Some modern-day foragers and wild food enthusiasts have revived Native American practices regarding the roasted bay nut.

More so than many other species of tree that is part of the Southern Pacific coastal area, the bay laurel adapts well to varied conditions. It can be found on the bluffs overlooking the ocean, in canyons or on hills, within the shade of the redwood forest, or in the hot, dry chaparral. On top of the hills, and on dryer sites, it may grow as an understory tree or even appear as a shrub, but under the right conditions—along permanent sources of water—it can reach heights of eighty to one hundred feet, and have a crown that spans eighty feet or more.

Bay laurel also sprouts vigorously, with new shoots appearing from fallen trunks, as well as cut or damaged stumps. The base can be massive, and spread out until it reaches nearly fifty feet in circumference, with the trunks themselves sometimes over two feet in diameter.

The fruit is a round, green berry, lightly spotted with yellow, which matures purple. Under the thin, leathery skin, it has an oily, fleshy covering that surrounds a single hard, thin-shelled pit. Resembling a miniature avocado, the fruit ripens in late fall.

The flowers, which occur in late winter and early spring, are small, yellow and

< 74 >

< Secret Voices from the Forest >

grow in stalked *umbels*. They form an umbrella-like shape, giving rise to the genus name *Umbellularia*.

A member of the Laurel family, California bay laurel shares its family with Grecian laurel, mountain laurel, sassafras, cinnamon, and avocado.

In Oregon, the California bay laurel is known as Oregon myrtle. It has also been called Pepperwood, Spicebush, Cinnamon Bush, Peppernut Tree and Headache Tree.

Under whatever name, this hardwood is only found on the Southern Oregon and Northern California Coast. "Myrtlewood" is considered a world-class *tonewood*—wood that has is recognized to have consistent acoustic qualities when used in the construction of musical instruments—and is sought after by makers of violins and guitars from around the world.

Myrtlewood is the only wood still in use as a base "metal" for legal tender. In the depths of the Great Depression, between Franklin Roosevelt's election and his inauguration, The First National Bank, in the town of North Bend, Oregon was forced to temporarily close its doors. As this was the only bank in town, its closing created a cash-flow crisis for the City of North Bend.

The city took matters in hand and began minting its own currency, using myrtlewood discs printed on a newspaper press. These coins, in denominations from 25¢ to $10, were used to make payroll and the city promised to redeem them for cash as soon as it became available.

However, when the bank reopened and the city asked people to bring their myrtlewood money in to redeem it, many decided to keep their tokens as collector's items. After several appeals, the city gave up, announcing that the tokens would remain legal tender in the city of North Bend in perpetuity. Until the 1960s, people occasionally did cash in their tokens, but the remaining pieces have become very valuable through scarcity and historical interest. Fewer than ten full sets are believed to exist.[23]

‹ Southern Pacific Coast : Mediterranean Chaparral and Riparian Woodlands : Bay Laurel ›

CALIFORNIA BAY LAUREL COMPANIONS

Scarlet Frittilary
California Whipsnake
Alder Borer
Mission Bells

Blue Blossom Tree
Giant Swallowtail
Western Azalea
Pacific Tree Frog
Leccinum Manzanitae

Catalina Ironwood
American Avocet
Sacramento Perch
Golden Stars

Northern Elephant Seal
Baby Blue Eyes
Anna's Hummingbird
White Globe Lily
Western Grey Squirrel

I keep secure among my many
 dark trunks, a palace
for the loves
and pleasures
of shadows
to which the wind brings news
from ancient coastal cities
far away.

Heroes and gods have set down
at my foot sandal and spear
and crossed inside;
my leaves like beaten bronze
have tamed the sun.

The wind brings news . . .
when it can find me.

FACTS ABOUT SOME LAUREL COMPANIONS

Anna's Hummingbird

Anna's is the most common species of hummingbird in southern California, and one of only three species that are permanent residents of the U.S. and Canada, along with Allen's and Costa's. Chaparral is their favored habitat, although they can nest and thrive in many different environments, including open woods. However, with the expansion of suburban development, their range has increased dramatically, as they find food throughout the year in suburban gardens with feeders and exotic plantings.

Hummingbirds do not normally make song; rather, they chirp and make deep-throated guttural sounds, communicating with each other via visual displays. Unusually, Anna's Hummingbird is considered to have a minimal song. This vocalization is part of the male Anna's dramatic, and distinctive, courting display.

He flies high, up to 150 feet, then rapidly dives, pulling out a few feet from the object of his attentions with an explosive squeak. After hovering and singing for the benefit of the beholder, he may repeat this display over a dozen times.

It has been discovered that the "dive noise" is supplemented by the fluttering of the bird's outer tail-feathers, which work much the same as the reed of a saxophone. The feathers vibrate, producing a chirping sound much louder than what is emitted by its voice box, which is called a *syrinx*.[24]

Pacific Tree Frog

This is the only western frog whose call is a "ribbit." A frog calls in the spring while looking for mates.

The call of the Baja California treefrog is known throughout the world through its wide use as a nighttime background sound in old Hollywood movies, even those set in areas well outside the range of this frog.

The call of the Baja California treefrog is identical to that of the Sierran treefrog and the Northern Pacific treefrog, and it is possible that the calls of any of these species were used as movie sound effects.[25]

< 78 >

< Secret Voices from the Forest >

Blue Blossom Tree

This is the hardiest and largest *ceanothus*. Each spring the highways of the West coast display masses of blue blossom flowers, resembling lilacs. The scientific name, meaning "thyrse-flower," refers to the compact, branched flower cluster. *Thyrsus* is the name of the staff, adorned with leaves and berries that belonged to Bacchus, the Greek God of wine.

The California Indians used the flowers as soap, as they produce a fine lather when rubbed on the skin. The roots produced a red dye, the seeds were eaten, the leaves were dried and smoked with tobacco, and both the flowers and leaves were used to make tea.

Northern Elephant Seal

Elephant seals derive their name from their great size and from the male's large proboscis, which is used in making extraordinarily loud roaring noises, particularly during the mating competition.

A bull will typically have a harem of thirty to one hundred cows, depending on the size and strength of the bull. Over its lifetime, a successful bull could easily sire over five hundred pups, whereas most bulls will never mate, due to the hierarchy established by combat.

Elephant seals are renowned for their ability to remain submerged for very long periods of time. They dive to great depths while feeding—one thousand feet to nearly half a mile, on average. The northern elephant seal can dive deeper and longer than a sperm whale, stay submerged for up to two hours, and reach depths of more than a mile. The seals repeat these dives almost continuously for two to eight months and spend 80-95 percent of their time at sea submerged.

The seals have the ability to stop blood flow to areas of the body that may not require it during a dive and preferentially send it to the brain and heart, which are hypoxia-sensitive tissues. Scientists know the seal is also capable of shutting down blood flow to the kidneys during the dive. The seal breathes out during the dive down, and by about 100 feet, its lungs are collapsed.[26]

Western Grey Squirrel

A common misconception is that grey squirrels bury nuts in autumn and then remember where the nuts are when they need them in winter. However, according to the *National Audubon Society Field Guide to Mammals*, grey squirrels relocate their hidden caches by scent, not memory.

The squirrel has the ability to smell nuts through a foot of snow. When the snow is deeper, the animal tunnels down until it can pick up the scent and dig out the precious nut. The grey squirrel recovers as many as 85 percent of all the nuts it buried the prior autumn.[27]

Western Azalea

There are two kinds of azaleas: *native* species, a plant that can reproduce from seed, and hybrids, or *cultivars*, which can only be propagated by cloning, using cuttings from another plant. Azalea lovers have created hybrids for hundreds of years, producing over ten thousand different cultivars.

The azalea is a part of the genus *Rhododendron*. Although evergreen azaleas occur in other parts of the world, all native North American species are deciduous, and occur in a variety of colors. There are seventeen species native to North America, but only *Rhododendron occidentale* occurs naturally in the Pacific Northwest. The rest are native to the eastern half of the continent.

From 1849 to 1853, the Veitch Nurseries of Exeter, England, sent plant collectors all over the world to acquire new species and their seeds to expand their commercial nurseries. In North America, William Lobb obtained samples of the western azalea, which became an early contributor in the development of deciduous hybrid azaleas in Great Britain.

He also obtained samples from bristlecone and other pines unknown in Great Britain, as well as many other tree species. Finally, encountering the mighty sequoia, he cut the expedition short. He renamed the tree *Wellingtonia gigantea*, in honor of the Duke of Wellington, although the name is invalid under the botanical code.[28]

< 80 >

< Secret Voices from the Forest >

Flower Jewel Beetle

Beetles first appeared during the lower Permian period, about 240 million years ago.

They are the dominant form of life on earth, constituting almost one-quarter of all known life forms. There are more than 350,000 described species of beetles worldwide, thirty thousand of which have been identified as North American species. This represents nearly forty percent of all known insects.

Beetles are found on land and in fresh water. However, while they can adapt to almost any environment, they are not known to occur in the sea or in the regions near the poles.

Coleoptera is the largest order in the animal kingdom, containing a third of all insect species. Aristotle described beetles as insects with wing cases, thus *Coleoptera*, from Greek *koleos*, meaning "sheath," and *pteron*, which means "wing."

Species in this order are characterized by a hard exoskeleton and hard forewings called *elytra*, features that protect the hindwings, which are used for flying. This elytra separates beetles from most other insect species, except for a few members of the order *Hemiptera*, often known as the "true bugs." The elytra are often brightly colored and patterned, earning these creatures the epitaph "living jewels."[29]

< 81 >

Catalina Ironwood

Catalina ironwood, officially known as the *Lyontree*, is in the rose family. It is native to the Channel Islands of California, where it grows in the chaparral and oak woodlands of the rocky coastal canyons. Indians made the tough wood, known locally as ironwood, into spear handles and shafts, and European settlers used it for making fishing poles and canes. It is alone in a distinct genus.

Fossil studies suggest that there were once several other species within this genus, growing on the mainland—all but one now extinct. However, it is not an endangered species, as it is widely cultivated as an ornamental.

< Southern Pacific Coast : Mediterranean Chaparral and Riparian Woodlands : Bay Laurel >

TUBS AND THE SNAKE

When I first moved to New Mexico from Missouri in 1997, I brought along my cats—all seven of them . . . yes, I know. Four black ones: Peeps, Tubs, Ralph, and Fuzzy, a little white butterball named Fats, a one-eyed grey lady called Mags, and Rosebud, a hardy old tortie, who lived to be twenty-four, probably because of her perpetually crabby attitude.

For their own safety, in urban areas, I had always kept them indoors. So when I moved into my partially finished house on the mesa outside Taos, I thought it would be nice for them to get to roam around a bit, and I began letting them go outdoors for part of the day.

That only lasted for a year or two, as interaction with nature became an issue.

My home is literally plunked down in the middle of nowhere, many miles from any town, an off-grid straw-bale house that took me ten years of little-bit-by-little-bit construction to finish, most of it with my own hands. (I will understand if the character of "Maggie" springs to mind, to those of you who remember Adam's sarcastic description of her, from "Northern Exposure.")

A few other people live nearby, although none any closer than a half mile, so the local wildlife is as much a part of the neighborhood as humans. There are pronghorn antelope, the occasional elk, the ubiquitous coyote, once a rumored black bear, and rodents by the doubtless millions—of nearly endless variety, including both jackrabbits and cottontail bunnies. Then there are the birds: ravens, bluebirds and mourning doves, flycatchers, quail and three kinds of hummingbirds, owls that you hear but almost never see, finches and sparrows, and a flashy yellow and orange something I saw pass through a couple of times. There are also tarantulas, and to go along with them, tarantula hawks—particularly large, ferocious, orange-winged wasps that lay their eggs inside tarantulas' live bodies. Eewww.

Then there are the rattlesnakes.

I grew up in the country, but I must have been pretty sheltered, because I don't think I ever saw anything more intimidating than the black snake that was permitted permanent residence in the oat bin of the horse barn, there to deter mice and rats.

I have to tell you, when you see your first six-foot long rattler, curled up on the front step, you suddenly understand the age-old ancestral fear of wild things. And let's not fool ourselves—everything out there *really is* out to get us! Not with malice, of course, but hey, ya gotta eat, right?

Letting the cats out created some difficulties, because cats, as carnivores, will hunt any small thing (living or not) that moves. So I never did let them stay out past dark, because I knew that once they had fixated on some mouse or rabbit, I'd never be able to get them to come back indoors, which would, in turn, make them easy pickings for the owls and coyotes.

One summer day, I was working on a stained glass project at my desk. The door was open and the cats were enjoying the morning sunshine. About eleven o'clock, a brief picture came into my mind—Tubs facing a big rattlesnake. As I say, brief—the mental picture lasted for all of one second, so I continued working. I kept the television's volume fairly high most of the time, so, a few hours later, when a sound like shotgun pellets in a dried gourd drowned out the noise from the TV, I was startled. After turning the set off, I looked out the window for the source of this racket: there was Tubs, two feet from a huge rattler, just as the scene had appeared in my mind a few hours earlier. I froze. If Tubs moved suddenly, she'd be struck in the face, and would very likely die from the bite. Fortunately, after a minute, she slowly and cautiously backed away from the snake, which slithered off into the brush.

But I didn't let it go at that. I knew the snake had made its nest near the house, so there was potential of a repeat performance. I went out, found the snake's hiding place, and dispatched it.

There was at least one other time that I chose to kill a snake—it had claimed my door-step as its favorite spot for an afternoon sunbath, where it naturally got into a confrontation with another of the cats. Then there were the unnerving occasions when baby rattlers found their way into the house, curling up under the refrigerator or the bookcase—but those I had captured and transported a couple of miles away.

Later, I was nagged by a persistent sense of guilt about killing something whose home I had invaded. After all, I alone am capable of making the decision to locate to an area that is not paved over and tamed. Living remotely has the advantages of peace and silence, as well as a freedom from the sometimes iron grip of neighborhood obeisance, but "civilized" man, or woman, is unaccustomed to the often life-threatening vagaries of nature. This was the animal's home first, and I had no right to punish him for my choice to put myself in the middle of an ecosystem in which I have no natural part to play.

So my solution was to stop letting the cats go out all together. I built them big fenced catteries, as I'd done at other locations. After all, the domestic cat is not a native of North America, its ancestors being originally from North Africa. It doesn't belong here.

I also made a promise to Big Snake in the Sky that I would never again intentionally kill one of His (or Her) children. Then, as a symbolic gesture, I put a framed painting of snakes on my wall. Since then, everybody inside and out has been happy.

CHAPTER THREE

THE PACIFIC COAST RANGES AND
THE GREAT BASIN

swift cloud shadow mottles
the towering cliff
a grain of sand settles

≫≫≫≫≫≫≫≫≪≪≪≪≪≪≪≪

THE PACIFIC COAST RANGES—INCLUDING THE CASCADES AND SIERRA NEVADA AND THE MONTANE FORESTS OF THE GREAT BASIN

The planet Earth is a ball of rock and metal, composed of four differing layers.

• At the very center, the **inner core** is solid, because it is under such pressure—as much as 45 million pounds per square inch.

• The **outer core** is in a liquid state. Both inner and outer cores are composed predominantly of nickel and iron, and range in temperature from 4000 to 9000 degrees F.

• The **mantle** is the thickest layer, and is made up of very hot, compressed rock, which has the ability to flow. Scientists believe that the difference in temperatures from top to bottom creates convection currents, which allow the crust to move.

• The **crust** is the outermost layer, and the thinnest. The crust floats on top of the mantle. It is composed of basalt, which constitutes the oceanic crust, and granite, which makes up most of the continental crust. Granite is lighter and less dense than basalt, so the continents ride on top of the oceanic crust.

Since the Earth's outer crust is so much thinner than the layer beneath, it easily fragments into segments, called *tectonic plates*. They are constantly moving against one another, in a variety of ways—sometimes horizontally, but sometimes one plate slides underneath another. These motions are also responsible for earthquakes and the formation of mountains, which then become part of the arrangement of the physical features of a continent, called the *topography*.[1]

The Pacific Coast mountain ranges, including the Sierra Nevada and the Great Basin, are part of an interactive section of the North American continent. These natural geological features, and their relationship, form the topography of this section of the Intermountain West.

The Continental Divide runs the entire length of the Americas, from Cape Prince of Wales, Alaska, to Tierra del Fuego at the southernmost tip of South America. In North America, the water east of the Divide flows to the Gulf of Mexico and the Atlantic Ocean. The water to the west flows toward the Pacific Ocean.

The exceptions to this rule are closed drainage basins, which have been formed by mountains or other natural geologic land formations. The Great Basin is such a system.

< 86 >

< Secret Voices from the Forest >

Imagine a large sink — *a 200,000 square mile sink* — that is set between mountains on every side. All precipitation in the region evaporates, seeps underground or flows into lakes, as there is no outlet to the sea. The inland water flows into dry watersheds, where the water evaporates, leaving a high concentration of salts and other minerals in the basin. Over time, these lakes become relatively saline, as well as more sensitive to environmental pollutants. This type of area is considered a desert biome — generally dry, with most precipitation arriving as snow.

The Great Basin includes most of Nevada, half of Utah, and sections of Idaho, Wyoming, Oregon, and California. The region is actually made up of many small basins, including the Great Salt Lake. It also contains the highest and lowest points in the contiguous United States — Death Valley and Mt. Whitney.[2]

Water vapor in the atmosphere becomes precipitation, eventually returning to the atmosphere through evaporation from the surfaces of land or water, or by *transpiration* from plants. This is a process by which a plant releases moisture, similar to sweating in animals.

Warm air blows in from the ocean towards the coastal mountains. The winds are forced upwards, the air cools, and the moisture falls back out as precipitation on the ocean side.

On the lee side of the mountain, the air descends, warms, and dries out. Roughly stated, the result may be that while great forests are on one side of the mountains, a desert will be present on the other.

Since all life on this planet depends on water to survive, 1) when and where it gathers, and 2) in what quantity, are two major factors that help to determine the type and variety of species of plants and animals found in any particular region.

< 87 >

The mountain ranges of the West consist of a number of more or less parallel chains, made up of nearly a hundred separately named ranges, and twelve major ice fields. They stretch along the West Coast of North America from Alaska south to Northern and Central Mexico. The Coastal Ranges are rugged, geologically young mountains formed by faulting and folding. North of San Francisco, the ranges are humid and thickly forested; the southern parts are dry and covered with brush and grass.[3]

The Sierra Nevada borders the Great Basin on the west. The primitive Sierras began forming when the Pacific Oceanic plate forced its way beneath the North American plate. The friction from this was so great that horizontal plumes of molten rock formed deep underground, structuring the base of the mountains. After that, a combination of volcanic and glacial activity, spanning one hundred million years, sculpted the spectacular scenery of the Yosemite Valley, King's Canyon and Sequoia National Parks, and Lake Tahoe.

< Pacific Coast Ranges and the Great Basin >

≼ INCENSE CEDAR ≽

REFLECTIONS ON SILENCE

What Incense Cedar Can Tell You About Itself

I find *Silence* to be a sense of stillness, full of presence and emotion, of possibility and excitement. I recognize it in the mountains—they are so *much*.

If I can, I will choose to be near them, surrounded by their massive, eternal substance. The mountains lend security and a sense of home to those of us whose lives are shorter and more easily extinguished. Here, the cool, sharp air accepts my fragrant gifts—a contribution to this place of rejuvenating tranquility.

My favorite time is winter. When snow blankets the world, occluding the noises of life, the silence becomes even more profound. Within this quiet place, awareness moves in further, but also expands to encompass all things, as they are also an extension of that core. If one wish could be granted me, I would want to be something, or somewhere that shares that in-between space, as *it* is *really* the Source of all.

It is my nature to transmit an impression of mystery and romance. I make you wonder what it would be like to travel and seek new experiences. These may not seem to relate, but the search for adventure can be an externalization of the qualities of silence—as the soul becomes still and its attention completely focused, it simultaneously becomes more acutely aware of the relation it has to its surroundings.

As for myself, I dream about the places the wind takes my scent, and how the atmosphere changes with our arrival.

Incense Cedar's Place in the World

It is a member of the Cypress Family. This family adapts, fitting into what space is allowed them. They are gentle and humble, moving aside for more impetuous forces. Incense Cedar is special for the locations it has chosen—for views of the magnificence that the essence of Spirit can make manifest.

When it talks to other trees, it speaks of reflections—of their own natures, through relation to each other, of the essence of things that pass by, as everything becomes affect of what comes near it, of the forces of the planet on the air and the sky (and what falls from it).

It stands at attention, and waits . . . for the future, about which we do not know, and for fate, about which we do not *want* to know.

It moves back and forth between a state of awareness of the physical dimension and a meditative cognizance of the ethereal nature of life, with an ease that is reflected in the graceful movement of its foliage . . . although, as in meditation, awareness of the core of Silence can be a fragile sensation. Easy to lose, easy to wander from . . . distracted, as the wind moves throughout branches, many armlets swaying together in response . . . distracted, as snow lays a blanket across the canopy, creating sheltering caverns for birds and mice—and below, for deer and elk to graze.

Incense Cedar's Message for Us

The Earth's energy is in a process of drawing together, becoming clearer, like an image coming into focus. This energy is driven by desire, which is not really dissatisfaction, but a necessary motivating force.

Matter pretends it is moving by using time to pass through space. Sometimes, to give itself the sensation of changing position, it blinks. This can be as simple as a single creature passing out of one physical form into another, or as profound as the beginning or ending of an Ice Age.

In the past, you have felt that you lacked color, and envied those creatures embodying it—not realizing that bright patterns and showy behaviors were aspects of survival, rather than ego. Much borrowing of finery has been the result, to compensate for this perceived lack.

The luminosity of Spirit manifests in all things. The task is to discern this. If you can capture the essence of each thing as it passes you, and incorporate that into the flesh of your body, you will be, in truth, all things, but remain one unto yourself.

Time for a new perspective—validate yourselves. See the innate beauty of the human animal, whatever its physical attributes.

The role of humans in the evolution of the life of this planet is to be a magnifying glass. You investigate everything in such minute detail, more so all the time. Eventually, you will arrive at the empty space between all things, where the Silence dwells.

Within the Silence is a sense of great peace and protection, no matter what may come in the world, and regardless of how the future resolves itself. This is not blindness to circumstance, or a giving-in to the inevitable, but a graceful passage through one's allotted time in existence.

Your avatars and wise men understood that listening promotes *true* awareness of all things, not just self. But even the avatars advance, so let go of the past.

CHRONICLES

The incense cedar's species name, *calocedrus decurrens*, means "beautiful cedar." This tree is not a true cedar, but a member of the Cypress family, although there are some resemblances. It was named for the cedar-like scent that is emitted by its wood. The crushed leaves are also fragrant, as is the resin when burnt. Incense cedar has aromatic wood that resists insects and decay. Practically no pests attack the tree, but in the forests where it is native, mature tree trunks are often infested with dry-rot of the heartwood.

In its younger years, especially when growing in the open, incense cedar forms an almost geometrically perfect pyramid, its lower branches nearly touching the ground. The whole mass is so densely overlapping that it sheds both rain and snow. In old age, after battling the elements for perhaps a thousand years, it can become much more irregular and picturesque, often with several crowns competing to replace the old one destroyed long before by lightning or wind.

True cedars are native to the Middle and Far East and North Africa, although some of these have been introduced to and thrive in North America.

It is a large evergreen that has the potential to reach heights of nearly 200 feet and a diameter of nine feet. It has reddish brown, flaky bark with long, deeply furrowed ridges, and fan-like branches that overlap in flattened, aromatic sprays. John Muir's observation of the incense cedar was, "No waving fern-frond . . . is more beautiful in form & texture, or half so inspiring in color & spicey fragrance."

Both sexes of flowers occur on the same tree, emerging from the ends of the leaf sprays. The female flowers develop into unusual-looking cones. Each cone produces two-winged seeds that can travel some distance on the wind. In nature, the incense cedar only spreads by seed.

Although slow growing, the incense cedar can survive more than five hundred years in the wild. This tree occurs naturally in areas with very dry summers—less than one inch of precipitation per month—and is considered remarkably heat and drought tolerant. This tolerance is attributed to the fact that this tree has an extensive, well-developed root system that spreads farther out than that of many other trees. This enables it to survive drought, as well as have resistance to strong winds. Incense cedar is also somewhat tolerant of frost, as well as injury from ozone.

It is also frequently planted to control erosion because it has a well-developed root system, with widely spreading lateral roots and several downward-growing roots. Both lateral roots and taproots have abundant branches, occupying a broad lateral area with depth.

Incense cedar has been widely cultivated as a bird and wildlife-friendly ornamental hedge, screen, or windbreak.

Because of its habit of growing close to the ground in its youth, many animals find shelter beneath its boughs.

Owls and other raptors build nests in older trees and as many species of insects are found on incense cedar, a large variety of insect-eating birds find food among its foliage. Relatively few of these insects cause serious damage to the tree.

The cedar wood wasp, a species that has remained unchanged for millions of years, uses the tree as a breeding ground. It lays its eggs in the tree immediately after forest fires, often when the wood still smolders, and the larvae develop inside the tree.

Incense cedar was used by the Cahuilla Indians of California to construct conical-shaped bark houses that were used for temporary shelter during acorn gathering times in late fall. In some areas, incense-cedar slabs were used in more permanent house construction. The Pomo Peoples of Mendocino County, California used the leaves of incense cedar in the process of leaching acorn meal and in a decoction for relieving stomach upset. Small limbs were sometimes used for bows, and twigs for brooms.[4]

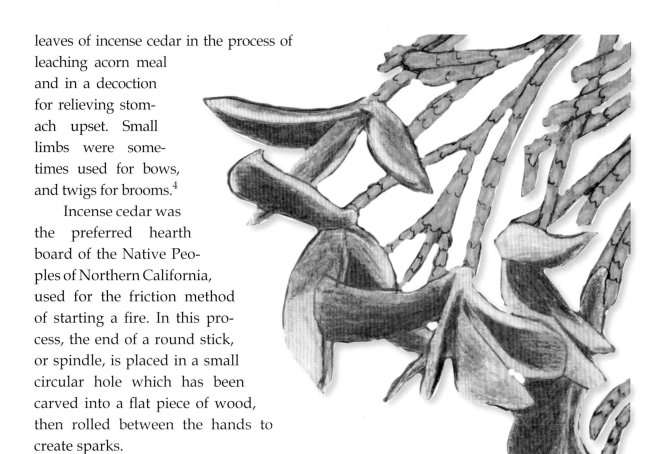

Incense cedar was the preferred hearth board of the Native Peoples of Northern California, used for the friction method of starting a fire. In this process, the end of a round stick, or spindle, is placed in a small circular hole which has been carved into a flat piece of wood, then rolled between the hands to create sparks.

There is still interest in this ancient practice, particularly amongst survivalists, who believe that society will in some way be interrupted in the future. They prepare for this possibility by having emergency medical training, stockpiling food and water, becoming self-sufficient, building structures that will help them survive, and learning old-fashioned practices that do not involve modern technology.[5]

Another common tradition among American Indian tribes was *smudging*, the burning of fragrant resins, herbs and other plants that were tied into a bundle. The resulting smoke was believed to be capable of purifying a dwelling or giving focus to a meditation or ritual.

Smudging is still a common practice today, and bundles of sage and other herbs can be found in most natural food stores or anyplace that sells incense. Many are decorated with dried flowers and colored ribbons.

For those wishing to make their own smudge sticks, traditionally, the most common plant that makes up a bundle is dried white sage. However, any fragrant, non-toxic herb growing in a stalk, such as lavender, sweetgrass, rosemary, thyme, juniper, or incense cedar, can be used as well.

INCENSE CEDAR COMPANIONS

Cobra Lily
Tiger Moth
Red-sided Shiner/Spotted Dace
Many-flowered Stickseed

American Pika
Western Peony
Spotted Towhee
Coffeeberry
Leopard Frog

Long-nosed Lizard
Harlequin Lupine
Cedar Wasp
Glistening Inkcap

Naked Broomrape
Shrike
Meadow Rue
Caribou
Alpine Saxifrage

In some level valley
where a river flows
will I put roots and there grow
foliage laden with resin,
dark as tourmaline,
liquid as beryl.
Thick and fragrant my bark
like heavy spice
brought across oceans.

In no kingdom on earth
have I and my sisters not grown;
we have held up
the houses of gods.
And so I will tell a thing:
the lifting sweep of our arms
cradles a womb of silence
where all that is is made.
It can't be seen, yet look
    where all the living creatures of the wood
        take shelter by it.

FACTS ABOUT SOME INCENSE CEDAR COMPANIONS

Western Peony

This nodding, maroon-colored flower is found among the sagebrush and open pine forests of Wyoming and Utah. Remaining dormant over the dry summer, after the winter snows, the flower develops prominent seedpods at its center. The flowers never open completely, maintaining a cupped shape.

While this species is not edible, American Indians used various parts of the plant for medicinal use. The root was ground to a powder and used as a remedy for colds, sore throat, and lung ailments. A tea, in small doses, purportedly relieved stress, depression, and menstrual pain.

There is evidence that peonies were used extensively in both the Far East and Europe as long as two thousand years ago. Peonies were used during medieval times to cure gallstones and jaundice, control epileptic seizures, to soothe teething pain, to aid in childbirth and to ward off evil spirits. Seeds were swallowed whole to prevent bad dreams, or made into a poultice to relieve a stomachache. Dried flower petals made a tea that was reputed to soothe a cough. Peonies were essentially considered a panacea.

Today a number of medical researchers throughout the world are isolating compounds in peonies and evaluating their medical potential. The peonies grown for medicinal use today are harvested for their root, and come almost exclusively from China, Korea and Taiwan.[6]

American Pika

Native to cold climates, the pika is a small rodent that lives around rocky slopes and boulder fields. Intolerant of high temperatures, it can die from overheating within a few hours.

It spends the day eating or storing grasses and other plants in hay piles, which is its food for the winter. Although the pika weighs on average about three and a half ounces, it must collect more than sixty pounds of hay to survive the winter. Like its rabbit relations, it only partly digests its food the first time through, later eating its own waste for its further nutritive value.

Pikas live in colonies, but members of the American species each have separate territories, which are actively defended. They are normally vigilant to the presence of predators, barking to warn other animals of danger. However, during disputes over hay-theft, they often open themselves up to attacks by ferrets or raptors.[7]

Cobra Lily

The name "cobra lily" stems from the similarity in appearance of its tubular leaves to a rearing cobra. They resemble fangs or a serpent's tongue. This variety of pitcher plant is carnivorous, and lures its insect prey with a sweet smell inside the leaf opening. Once inside, an insect is unable to escape because of the smooth surface of the inner tube and the sharp, downward pointing hairs.

As these plants usually grow in nutrient-poor, acidic bogs, insects are a nutritional supplement. It was once believed that this species did not produce any digestive enzymes, relying on symbiotic bacteria and protozoa to break down the captured insects into easily absorbed nutrients. Recent studies have indicated that the cobra lily secretes at least one enzyme that digests captured prey. The cells that absorb nutrients from the inside of the pitcher are the same as those on the roots that absorb soil nutrients.[8]

Loggerhead Shrike

This bird has a hooked beak, which it uses to kill insects, lizards, mice, and birds. The Loggerhead Shrike has developed the innovative behavior of impaling its catch on thorns or barbed wire. As it does not have strong feet or talons, this may help the bird rip up its prey or cache it for a future meal. Its nickname is the "Butcher Bird."

Naked Broomrape

This is a member of a group of parasitic plants mostly native to the temperate Northern Hemisphere. Its stems contain no chlorophyll, so their stems are yellow to straw colored, although its snapdragon-like flowers can be blue, white, or yellow. When they are not in flower, no part of the plant is visible above the soil surface.

As it is totally dependent upon other plants for survival, its seeds can remain dormant for many years until stimulated by chemical compounds released by living plant roots. The seeds then attach themselves to the host, developing tubers. Some commercial crops, like tomato, potato, pepper and beans, when infested by certain naturalized species of broomrape, can be completely destroyed, so the USDA placed it on the Federal Noxious Weed List in 2006.

The name came from the Latin *rāpum* (underground stock of a tree) *genistae* (broom, as it was noticed that the plant formed tubers on the roots of the broom plant.)

The Plantagenet kings used common broom (known as "*planta genista*" in Latin) as an emblem and took their name from it. It was originally the emblem of Geoffrey of Anjou, father of Henry II of England. Wild broom is still common around Anjou, France.

In Welsh mythology, Blodeuwedd is the name of a woman made from the flowers of broom, meadowsweet and the oak, to be the wife of Lleu Llaw Gyffes. Her story is part of the Fourth Branch of the *Mabinogion*.[9]

Caribou

A member of the deer family, the caribou has been a major source of subsistence for peoples of the far north for thousands of years. They used all parts of the animal, as the Plains Indians did the American bison. Domestication may have started as early as three thousand years ago, during the Bronze Age. In parts of the world other than North America, it is called the reindeer.

This animal is built to handle cold. It has two layers of fur, a dense woolly undercoat and a longhaired overcoat made up of hollow, air-filled hairs, rooted in a thick layer of fat. Its nose has specialized bones that increase the surface air inside the nostrils. Water condensed from expired air and increased oxygen enrich the caribou's blood, enabling it to withstand cold more efficiently. The animal also has two separate circulation systems that prevent heat loss. The system of their legs is independent from that of the rest of the body, allowing the temperature of the body to be up to fifty degrees warmer.

In summer, the caribou eats grasses, birch and willow leaves, and other plants, including mushrooms, but its primary winter diet is lichen, or reindeer moss. In order to reach it, the caribou must dig through the ice and crusted snow. The footpads of its hooves, which in summer are sponge-like for extra traction on soft, wet tundra, adjust to winter conditions by shrinking and tightening, creating a sharp, hollow scoop.

Some North American caribou annual migrations are so great that they rival those of Africa's Serengeti Plain, and are the farthest of any terrestrial mammal. They can travel distances of three thousand miles a year, and their territory covers an area of nearly four hundred thousand square miles. Part of the reason for this is that the lichen that they favor as food takes years to grow back, once eaten, so they must move to find more.

In most caribou populations, both sexes grow antlers, but lose them at different times of the year, the males losing theirs in winter. According to the myth, flying reindeer pull Santa Claus's sleigh. In the 1823 poem, "A Visit from St. Nicholas," they have all been given male names, and it has since been remarked that Santa's reindeer were unlikely to actually have been male, because they possessed antlers in the winter.[10]

Glistening Inkcap

This is a common edible fungus found all over the world. It grows in dense clusters on rotting hardwood and disturbed ground sites. Under humid conditions, it can also grow indoors on rotting wood. In one instance it was discovered about four hundred feet underground in an abandoned coal mine, growing on wooden gangways and props used to support the roof. The glistening inkcap can be highly productive, with several successive crops appearing during one fruiting season.

The entire cap surface is covered with reflective cells that look like flakes of mica, which give this mushroom its name.

It is edible, and is enjoyed in omelets and sauces. Nutritionally, it contains a very high concentration of potassium, but also accumulates heavy metals from exposure, so it should not be collected from roadsides and other areas that may be exposed to pollutants.

The scientific community has found the *Coprinellus micaeus* of interest since 1601, when it was the subject of a monograph by Carolus Clusius in *The History of Rare Plants*. As this mushroom is plentiful and easily grown in laboratories, it has often been the subject in studies of cells and the processes of spore production.

Bioactive compounds have been isolated from *Coprinellus micaeus*. One was found to inhibit the enzyme that aids cancer cells to resist chemotherapy, and one has been shown to have some modest potential as an antioxidant.[11]

Incense-cedar Wood Wasp

This is the only living member of a family that appears extensively in the fossil records of the Mesozoic era. It lays its eggs in the smoldering, charred wood of Incense cedar, red cedar, and juniper in the western United States and Canada. It is small, and rarely seen, except by firefighters.[12]

⪡ MOUNTAIN MAHOGANY ⪢

REFLECTIONS ON DISCOVERY

What Mahogany Can Tell You About Itself

My imperative is to find my way through the honeycombed holes in the fabric of space, to move towards the source of light. What is on the other side? I find that as I pass through one hole, another presents itself, and I must extend myself towards *it*. The holes are becoming . . . endlessly becoming. And I can do nothing but follow. Is there anything more important? Does it matter?

Perhaps it is because of the lights. When they're gone, the *urge* is gone—but only for a time, a waiting time. Then the lights return. Again, I have a purpose. The holes beckon, and I am once more becoming—following a glimpse of sky, a whiff of rain, an echo of wind.

Discovery, to me, is a Council of the Elders—the wisdom that comes from experience, implementing decisions that concern present actions. The fulfillment of dreams is only a filling of the holes with possibility. The inkling of what lies ahead is a reflection of the inner constitution, or innate nature. I don't think about Fate. It would be very dull to know what is going to happen before I even *want* something.

It seems to me that the wind does the same. How does it decide where to go next? It must know something I do not. I love catching the Wind unawares. It is used to me facing away, and sometimes gets bored with my constancy. During the brief times when its motion ceases, I turn around and, before it sees me, I move somewhere new and surprising. Ha! It is a good game.

Directional choices have to do with time, and a longing to be somewhere else. Does Time manifest because of our discontent? Or does discontent manifest because of Time?

The Future is Life . . . having an imagination.

Mahogany's Place in the World

Mahogany's ancestors passed on to it the knowledge that there are many ways of looking at survival. You can think of yourself as the long-suffering victim, or the warrior, or you can think of yourself as the wily competitor, finding a place for yourself in the world. My ancestors chose the latter. They learned to swallow light and moisture—the things they found when twisting through the holes. This, in turn, enhanced the urge to move and become.

They have been witness, many times, to a shift in the balance of fertility. There are less of some things and more of others, but that is the way the planet moves. It is like breathing in and out, except that the content of each breath is different from the last.

They like the view from the mountains—being halfway up—and can see many things. Although we may consider their surroundings barren, this species of tree finds them texturally rich. Their choice of location is also a manifestation of humility and a sense of closeness to the earth, of a nature that does not strive to go up high, or compete with others. Mountain Mahogany is modest, but not secretive. Like a pocket gopher, it has a respect for the brightness of daylight, but proceeds with the task of digging. As an explorer, it seeks the light, but the light is more a beacon towards the path, a direction to follow, than the thing being sought. It is the *action* of seeking that is important.

Mountain Mahogany is a member of the Rose Family, whose function in the world is Sharing. The specifics—location, and choice of beneficiaries—are what make the Rose Family unique. Their place in the world is like that of subterranean animals; they give texture to the support-structure of life.

Mountain Mahogany has learned to bow its head to keep in contact with the Earth. That way, it can see evolution happening from an insider's point of view.

Its dream is that it will one day explode into, and *become* Light.

Mountain Mahogany has realized that slow and steady may win the race, but luck does not hurt either. Be at the right place at the right time, and you will then have the choice of whether to be a part of things, or have them done to you.

Mahogany's Message for Us

< 102 >

You have the power to be controllers, or managers, when you do this well. By speeding up the natural course of events, you affect directions, although not necessarily outcomes. It would be helpful if you became aware that your behavior does *not* set you apart from all other aspects of life on this planet. You, like the rest of us, are a product of inner processes that dictate all, including conscious thought.

Do not be ruled by fear of things that have a different appearance.

Discovery manifests in you through seeking. You are *always* seeking, even when you seem to be burrowing into a place that does not shine with the light of adventure. Then you are attempting to find safety and security. In all cases, the emotions drive the actions, and the emotions, again, are a product of the inner processes.

Learn to watch yourself going with the flow. There will again come a time when the urge itself will be the only thing that is important to discover.

< Secret Voices from the Forest >

CHRONICLES

< 103 >

This shrubby, slow-growing tree is generally found on rocky mountain slopes, just before the pine forests begin, between altitudes of four thousand and eight thousand feet. It is usually an average of three to fifteen feet in height, but if left undisturbed, it can attain heights of at least forty feet. Ages of over 1300 years have been recorded. Some argue that this is the oldest known individual flowering plant (as opposed to a clone.) The fact that it is also evergreen is unusual in itself, considering the cold, arid conditions in which it occurs.

Evergreen leaves are usually hard and waxy, an adaptation that helps a flowering plant reduce water loss. The presence and frequency of flowering plants with evergreen leaves increases as the climate becomes warmer. As a result, the greater percentage of flowering evergreen plants are found in Mediterranean and tropical climates, while fewer evergreen flower species are prevalent in the cooler conditions of the temperate zones.

Vascular plants, those having tissue for conducting water, are of two types: 1) seedless — ferns, mosses, and horsetails, and 2) seeded. There are two types of seed plants: 1) *gymnosperms*, which means "naked seeds" — no flowers, sexual reproduction through an exposed seed; and 2) *angiosperms* — plants that flower during sexual reproduction, and whose seeds are enclosed in a fruit.

< Pacific Coast Ranges and the Great Basin : Mountain Mahogany >

Angiosperms make up 80 percent of the existing plant species. Angiosperms began to branch off from the older gymnosperms over two hundred million years ago. The first flowering plants date back 140 million years. After greatly diversifying, some sixty to one hundred million years ago, they overtook coniferous species as the dominant form of plant life.

Evergreen and *deciduous* are descriptive terms, but they are not part of the plant classification system, and seem to be a factor related more to location and climate. Although there are five times as many deciduous types of angiosperm, there are many species of evergreen angiosperms, such as mangrove and magnolia, and several other members of the Rose family. However, the general rule is that these other trees occur in climates where freezing temperatures are an infrequent occurrence, such as warm coastal areas or the southern North American desert.

Some adaptations the mountain mahogany has made to live in the cold and arid areas of the Great Basin are a generally small size, tough hard wood, short asymmetrical branches that reach *out* more often than *up* in order to cope with strong winds, and small leaves, with a waxy coating which conserves moisture.

The seeds of the fruits of the mountain mahogany have distinctive corkscrewing plumes that look like fuzzy pipe cleaners. In hot, dry weather, they often straighten out, curling again after it rains. This occurs both while on the plant, and after wind disperses the seed, which may help to drive the seed into the soil. The meaning of its scientific name, *Cercocarpus*, is "tailed fruit."

< 104 >

The curlleaf mountain mahogany isn't really a mahogany tree, but has been so named because its dense wood will not float in water, and its roots, bark, and reddish-brown, mahogany-colored heartwood can be used to make a red dye. It is a member of the Rose family.

Worldwide, the Rose family is large, containing nearly three thousand *known* species of trees, shrubs, and herbs. They are distributed over every continent except Antarctica, and it is assumed that there are many more species yet to be discovered. In North America, there are seventy-seven native species

< Secret Voices from the Forest >

of tree alone, including the toyon and Lyontree, mountain ash, crabapples, and many different species of cherry and plum.

The members of this family usually have showy, perfect five-petal flowers. The fruits are often edible, and have been hybridized into countless varieties over thousands of years of human cultivation.

After the Grass and Pea families, the Rose family is probably the third most economically important group of crop plants in the world, including apples, pears, quinces, loquats, almonds, peaches, apricots, plums, cherries, strawberries, raspberries, blackberries, boysenberries, loganberries, prunes, and cut roses.

Other members of the Rose family often occupy the same areas as mountain mahogany, in the form of shrubs. These include species of serviceberry and hawthorn, bitterbrush, wild blackberries and raspberries, potentilla, and the cliff rose.

Because the trunk and branches of mountain mahogany are short and twisted, it cannot be turned into lumber for building. Some Indian tribes carved shorter pieces of the heavy, close-grained wood into tool handles, weaving forks, fire sticks, ceremonial equipment, *camas* (or digging sticks), bows, fish spears and arrow points and, as the wood takes a high polish, occasionally flutes.

The Shoshoni, Navajo, Paiute, and other tribes used all parts of the plant for medicinal use: internally, for stomachaches, heart disorders, tuberculosis, diphtheria, pneumonia, and diarrhea; externally, for venereal diseases, treatment of burns or wounds, as an eyewash, and as a treatment for earaches.

The curlleaf mountain mahogany is an important source of food and shelter for many species of wildlife all year round. Mountain sheep and goats, elk, deer and antelope eat its leaves, flowers, fruits and bark, and many small mammals and birds, such as Blue Grouse, find cover within stands of this small, twisted tree.

In mature stands, most of the trees' foliage has become out of reach to browsing deer, but as it is an evergreen, it still provides protection from winter storms.[13]

< 105 >

< Pacific Coast Ranges and the Great Basin : Mountain Mahogany >

MOUNTAIN MAHOGANY COMPANIONS

Northern Shoveler
Scaly Pholiota
Spotted Langloisia
Nuttal's Sheepmoth

Sandberg Bluegrass
Kangaroo Rat
Skunkbush
Collared Lizard
Showy Thistle

Golden Yarrow
Long-nosed Snake
Kit Fox
Coyote Mint

Sage Grouse
Yerba Mansa
Lupine Blue Butterfly
Rosin Weed
Thistledown Velvet Ant

In the mountains, in the high air,
something electric, a molecular sparking,
pricking close and distant alike with clear
potential, pulling the leafshape, guiding
the subdividing cell, erecting through all the reaches
of space and the rolling of time a dense geometry
of leaf and vein, twig and stem, which weaves into its tale
as well other, accidental lights: the dull schisty glint
of a skidding stone, dislodged by bolting prey;
the ghostly flashing of a wave
from a sea no longer there

from where instead the winds
lean hard against the forming trunk
and have their shape set solid
in the flinty grain,
season after season,
bent like the prow
of a byegone
boat

as it might be
anchored to the broken earth
with roots like iron flukes; roots
warped and webbed among loose rock,
binding gravels, dendritic threading through sharp
shards of sand, feeling for the heat
of hematite, the domains of magnetite,
wired far into the sleeping land
as it dreams geologies

FACTS ABOUT SOME MOUNTAIN MAHOGANY COMPANIONS

Golden Yarrow

Yarrow has been used traditionally as a medicinal herb by early peoples of both North America and Europe, for a host of purposes. In ancient times, one of the uses for yarrow was to stop the flow of blood from wounds received in battle. Taught by the centaur Chiron, it was believed that the great warrior-hero Achilles was first to use the plant for this purpose. The plants generic name, *Achillea*, is a tribute to him.

Frequently occupying grasslands and open areas in forests, yarrow is a medium-sized perennial shrub that improves the health of sick plants when it grows near them, and attracts butterflies and ladybugs. Several different kinds of birds use it to line their nests. It is thought that they do so to keep parasites from becoming a nuisance.

Yarrow was one herb identified at Shanidar IV, a Neanderthal flower burial of northern Iraq, dated circa 60,000 BCE, along with a number of other medicinal herbs.[14]

Kit Fox

This is North America's smallest fox, no bigger than a small house cat, with large ears and grey-to-tan coloration that keeps it well camouflaged. The kit fox hunts at night, eating mostly small rodents, reptiles and birds. It favors arid climates and drinks no water, as it is provided with enough liquid from the bodily fluids of its prey.

Kit foxes live in multiple underground dens scattered around their territory, dug out of loose soils in open areas. Their dens, and nocturnal activity, are important adaptations to the dry climates in which they live. They move from one den to the other to avoid predators, such as coyote. Home territories often overlap, and foxes from different family groups hunt the same areas, but not simultaneously.

< 108 >

< Secret Voices from the Forest >

Yerba Mansa

This is another all-purpose medicinal aid used by the American Indians for both topical and internal infections, sore feet, venereal diseases, diaper rash, as a general pain remedy, a disinfectant, an anti-fungal, anti-bacterial, and an anti-inflammatory. It can also be eaten and made into beads.

A striking white flower having *bracts*—which are modified leaves, rather than petals—it favors marshy areas. As the plant ages, it develops red and purple stains, and the entire plant turns brick red in the fall.[15]

Collared Lizard

The collared lizard is so named for the two black stripes around its neck. It can reach a total length of up to fourteen inches—mostly tail, which it waves as it stalks its prey. Unlike many other species of lizard, whose tails will grow back if severed, the collared lizard's tail, once lost, is lost for good.

It is one of the few desert lizards that is bipedal, and can sprint quite quickly, around sixteen miles per hour.

Sandberg Bluegrass

A perennial native bunchgrass, it is an important part of the sagebrush grasslands of the West. Sometimes reaching four feet in height with a strong root system, it provides food for a variety of wildlife, particularly deer and the many species of rodents—beaver, marmot, squirrels, hares, rabbits, and prairie dogs—as well as cover for ground bird species, such as pheasant and Sage Grouse.

In the Great Basin and Intermountain West, fire is an important component of a healthy ecosystem. When they have well-established root systems and are not overgrazed, the wild grasses are the fuel that feeds fire, but they are not completely destroyed. When these grasses are no longer present, wildfires occur less often, but can still be catastrophic, leading to denuded land, extended drought and inhospitable conditions for plants and animals alike.

Sage Grouse

Sage Grouse are noted for their elaborate courting rituals, in which groups of males congregate and display together. They puff out air sacs in their chests, making a loud booming sound, spread their long, pointed tail feathers, and strut for the benefit of the breeding females. This performance lasts for several hours each morning and evening during the mating season.

Living, nesting and foraging on the ground in the sagebrush grasslands all year round, they eat sagebrush, grasses, flowers, and insects, rarely move great distances, and perform the mating rituals in the same locations year after year.

Coyote Mint

A native of the California cost ranges, coyote mint, with its purple, scented blooms that tolerate desert conditions well, is one of the favored wildflowers used in *xeriscape* gardens. This type of garden is becoming increasingly popular in the dry conditions that are the norm in a large part of the North American West. As once seemingly endless supplies of water disappear, efforts are being made to teach an expanding population about the wise use of one of our most precious resources.

Xeriscaping was a term coined in the 1970s in Denver, Colorado to mean water-wise or water-efficient landscaping. The term "xeriscape" is derived from the Greek *xeros*, which means "dry." That doesn't mean that the only plants in a water-efficient garden are cactus. One chooses plants that are appropriate to the climatic conditions of their site—no Kentucky bluegrass in the desert, for instance—and by so doing create a landscape that can be maintained with little or no supplemental watering.[16]

The Santa Fe Gardens in Santa Fe, New Mexico "specializes in drought tolerant, water-wise . . . plants that need little or no extra water once established."[17]

Thistledown Velvet Ant

The name of this insect is misleading, as it is actually a wasp, as one may discover if attempting to handle the wingless females. Males have wings, but no stingers, and both sexes escape predation by burrowing underground. If the ant is caught, it will emit a high-pitched squeaking alarm to startle predators, usually bats and owls.

It is covered with long white hairs that provide it with camouflage, as the hairs mimic those of creosote seeds. The Thistle-down Velvet ant is extremely elusive, so its numbers are difficult to determine.

Although the adult wasps feed primarily on the nectar from cactus flowers, the female deposits her eggs in the burrows or nests of other insects, particularly those of the sand wasp. When they hatch, the Velvet Ant's larvae eat the larvae of the other insect, as well as the food that has been brought by the host female wasp for her own larvae.[18]

Spotted Langloisia

The spotted langloisia, also known as the Great Basin langloisia or lilac sunbonnet, is a tiny, ground-hugging member of the Phlox family growing in dry gravelly places in deserts, among creosote bush, piñon and juniper. As its flowers are typically one half-inch across, it can be easily missed in its environment.

The Phlox family contains about three hundred species, most of them natives of North America. Several species are brightly colored, and the genus name, *Phlox*, is derived from the Greek word for flame. Garden phlox, or *Phlox paniculata*, originally a shade of dusky purple, was introduced to England in 1730. There it was transformed into the familiar garden flower of today, and is now available in shades of red, purple, pink or white. In the 1820s, a British naturalist brought seeds from a bright red species of Phlox named *drummondii* back to Europe. The plant was bred into a variety of colors, and forty years later, its cultivars returned with names like "Starfire" and "Prime Minister."

Members of the Phlox family are attractive to butterflies, bees, and hummingbirds, and those with pale-colored flowers draw moths and bats at night. Phlox can be tall, with thick, glossy leaves, or it can spread across the ground with needle-like leaves, as does the spotted langloisia. All forms have five petals on a tubular base.[19]

⪡ SEQUOIA ⪢

REFLECTIONS ON HEART OF THE WORLD

What Sequoia Can Tell You About Itself

The *Heart of the World* is a place deep within the planet that strives to be life manifest — it is the essential aspect of quickening. The core of the Earth is hot and moving, like blood, and like blood, it feeds the systems that make soil and water, clouds and weather. It pulls each thing towards itself, only to push that away and bring in more. It is an urge to *acquire* that creates movement.

Acting like a sponge, I have been soaking up the memories of the Earth as it has changed over time. My particular species will assist in the crossover time that is yet to come. I cannot tell you what the future will hold, or even if my species will be in attendance.

I dream about the space *between* — where lies the energy-source that dictates the differentiation of physical forms, connecting them, as each one comes into being. You may call this *dark matter*. It does not predetermine, but rather decides manifestation in relation to what has come before, including the possibility of forms or qualities that are diametric opposites. This is the essence of response. This quality of responsiveness is what you would call "God," but it is not supernatural, just bigger and more complicated than you.

It is important to me to watch and to perceive everything all at once, but I absorb the significance slowly, to lose no nuance. I do not have a front or back, so I "see" in all directions simultaneously. It is an interactive awareness of presence, or lack of it, by sensing spatial and motional variances.

I enjoy being in the mountains, as it enables one to look out over the whole world, or so it seems. I appreciate gravity, and knowing that things always roll *down*. Once I was a mote in the tail of a comet, which is how I came to be here in the first place.

Sequoia's Place in the World

We maintain a portion of the self-awareness of the planet — its bigness. While the mountains, the ocean, the land, and the planet itself are vastly larger, it is difficult for smaller beings to completely comprehend this quality. Among the plants and animals, some of us exemplify "big."

My kind is mindful of the atmosphere created within our realm. At the top, there is a great expanse of green that caresses the sky. At the base, among the steep slopes peopled by our massive presence, it is quiet and peaceful — a place of security and protection. This is a reflection, in its own way, of that hot inner core of the planet. Although it is a violent furnace, it is also by nature a self-contained and secure realm.

We have learned that *everything* having an element of motion within itself is a mini-version of this quality. Atoms whirl around a tiny core, uniting to create something larger . . . and so it goes on forever.

Since achieving consciousness has always been the plan, we, the Sequoia, are to act as sentinels as long as we can, to protect the advance of a New Age. The Earth itself experiences great changes—the ground has moved many times, covered long distances, altering the surface of the planet. But the biggest change has been the swings in temperatures, which can sometimes be disruptive to the goal. However, all things, all occurrences, give comfort to someone. It is a matter of perspective.

Sequoia's Message to Us

Humanity is like a spinning vortex, drawing the energy of the planet into itself, into a place that exists in the future—the unknown time. This is where you are creating another dimension, as your group-awareness slowly begins to rise above the cloud of the consciousness of life forms dealing with the physicality of existence.

Small particles of energy are drawn together through similar purpose and intent. They create cohesive forms that still carry the original, innate purpose of the smaller particles, but now they must struggle with the reality of physical existence, *which is the product of many, many cohesive forms in competition for the same space*. It is easy to get mired into the movement of this struggle, where the original motivational drive, *the need to be whole*, is clouded by the physical interpretation of that intention, which is *to have definition*.

That interpretation becomes fear and need for acquisition and control of everything that surrounds the form. But the consciousness of humans is slowly returning to the focus of the original intent, and bright lights appear above the cloud. The lights appear, and then fade; more appear, then again fade. This has been the case for only a short time–perhaps the lifetime of one of our oldest, but now the lights have begun to increase in number.

If humanity embraced the Sequoia's understanding of the connectivity of life on the planet, it could help eliminate guilt and fear, but this is an innate understanding that emerges in seedling form when one being sees another in pain or difficulty. This is a very personal sensation that can dramatically alter the core of an individual. It has the capacity to begin or further the transformation of one individual into a being of light—one of *those* lights.

In order to be elevated further, it is important to concentrate on *humility*. While humanity is the animal life form that is moving most rapidly towards its own transformation, it is also the one most capable of self-immolation. Instant by instant, continue moving beyond the physical aspect of the senses, with the intention of learning. The task is to comprehend, not just hear; feel, not just touch; connect, not just see.

< Secret Voices from the Forest >

CHRONICLES

The giant sequoia, as a species, is the largest living thing on earth. Its close relative, the coast redwood, is the tallest species, but has less volume. They are both of the Redwood family, and are cone-bearing conifers, but have many physical differences. For instance, the sequoia can live twice as long, up to *four thousand years*.

It also requires very different environmental conditions in which to survive: the coast redwood lives only along the Pacific coastline, in a humid climate, with frequent fog. The giant sequoias' native range is between five and eight thousand feet, along the western slope of the Sierra Nevada mountain range. The trees form groves in a narrow belt of favorable locations with rich soil and moderate precipitation that comes mostly in the form of snow. It is thought that the scarcity of the sequoia is due to the ravages of the great glaciers that scoured out the Valleys of the Sierra Nevada during the last ice age. Today, they occupy an area of only about 35,000 acres.

The giant sequoia has bark that is three times as thick as that of the coast redwood—up to thirty-six inches. This fibrous bark provides fire protection, which has been an important factor in the tree's survival. It does not thrive in shade, so periodic fires eliminate other trees in the environment, which may crowd out sequoia seedlings. Seed is the only means by which the sequoia regenerates. A large tree may have from ten thousand to forty thousand cones, containing an average of two hundred seeds each.

Cones hang on the tree green and remain closed for up to twenty years. Douglas squirrels or the larvae of a tiny cone-boring beetle

< 115 >

< Pacific Coast Ranges and the Great Basin : Sequoia >

may cause cones to open, but fire is the main agent in the dispersal of seeds. It causes the cone to dry, open, and drop its seeds. Fire also consumes logs and branches that have accumulated on the forest floor. Their ashes form fertile seedbeds that ensure seedbed fertility. [20]

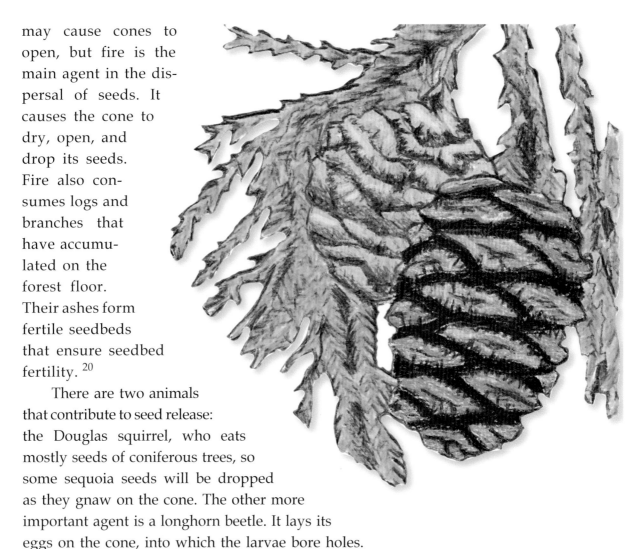

There are two animals that contribute to seed release: the Douglas squirrel, who eats mostly seeds of coniferous trees, so some sequoia seeds will be dropped as they gnaw on the cone. The other more important agent is a longhorn beetle. It lays its eggs on the cone, into which the larvae bore holes. This allows the cone to dry out and open, so that the seeds fall to the ground.

< 116 >

Giant sequoias do not gradually die of old age. The main cause of death for sequoias is toppling. Sequoias have a shallow root system with no taproot, so soil erosion, too much moisture, root damage, and strong winds can also lead to toppling. Sequoias can add one to two feet of height per year until they have reached between two hundred and three hundred feet high. After that, they will only increase in diameter.

It has been observed that the cone scales of the sequoia, arranged in ascending spiral rows, occur in a predictable pattern known as the Fibonacci Series or Golden Spiral—a series of numbers in which each number is the sum of the two preceding numbers. All plants with an alternate or spiral arrangement of leaves or scales exhibit patterns fitting the Fibonacci Series, and it is estimated that indeed 90 per cent of *all* plants have this arrangement.[21]

Through the tireless efforts of early conservationists like John Muir, these magnificent trees and their immediate environment have been protected. Established in 1890, Sequoia National Park is California's first national park and America's second oldest, receiving more than one million visitors per year.

< Secret Voices from the Forest >

The General Grant Tree is the only *living* national shrine, proclaimed so by President Dwight D. Eisenhower on March 29, 1956. Each year during the annual Christmas ceremony, park rangers place a large wreath at the base of the Grant Tree, to commemorate members of the American military who have given their lives in service to their country.

In the 18th century, Sequoyah, a highly respected Cherokee Indian, created a Cherokee language *syllabary*—which serves the purpose of an alphabet—that made reading and writing in Cherokee possible. It is the only time in recorded history that a member of an illiterate people independently created a new and effective writing system.

He was not a chief, as is commonly thought, but an inventive, skilled silversmith and farmer working in Georgia. In 1825, after the Cherokee Nation officially adopted his writing system, he went to Arkansas, where he set up a blacksmith shop and salt works, and taught his syllabary to anyone who was interested.

He was elected by the Cherokee Council in 1828 to be their representative in Washington, where he went to negotiate a treaty for land in Indian Territory. In 1838, the Cherokee were forcibly relocated on what was named "The Trail of Tears."

It was Sequoyah's dream to see his fragmented tribe reunited, and he died in about 1843 on a trip to Mexico, following reports that members of his scattered people were to be found there. The location of his grave is unknown. It has been generally assumed that the Sequoia tree was named in honor of this remarkable man.

A name used by the Mokelumne Tribe, in the Miwok tongue, was "Woh-woh'nau," or "Wawona." The word was apparently formed to imitate the hoot of an owl, which was considered the guardian spirit of the Sequoia trees. It was thought bad luck for anyone to cut or otherwise damage them.[22]

SEQUOIA COMPANIONS

Western Moss Heather
Mountain Lion
Sierra Nevada Ensatina
Bitter Cherry

Yellow-legged Frog
Canyon Live Oak
Spotted Bat
Common Camas
California Patch Butterfly

Golden Eagle
Snowbank Orangepeel Fungus
Arrowleaf Groundsel
Yosemite Toad

Mustang Linanthus
Twelve-spotted Skimmer
Monument Plant
Dark-eyed Junco
Canyon Dudleya

When the young boy goes in his Grandfather's
car to look at the tree, it feels ordinary at first.
He knows about cars—the awkward tilt of the seats,
the plush plastic smell—and about journeys; how scenes
slide past the glass as if on screens. They are mostly boring
interludes to be filled with dreamy imaginings.

But as the tone of the engine changes, and patches of sky appear
unexpectedly, and patches of white begin to temper the air; and
as the outside presses somberly round the car, darkening its
interior, he becomes still.

So that when the car door opens and he clambers out into the
cool, omnipresent sense of enduring strength, he is already half
entranced and walks shyly to the foot of the tree, his hands
clutched against his chest as though offering his own small life in
wondering comparison.

How can such bigness be? Such a rushing upward into the clouds;
such a plunging down to be the very shaft on which the whole
alive world slowly turns.

The boy doesn't feel the transition between gazing up with head
flung back and falling. He is only aware that the tree seems to be
laying itself down for him, becoming a bridge for him; a great road
for running on, with green caves and sweeping lights; his own,
forever road.

Then high concern is leaning over him; faces, branches, arms
reaching down. Amid gruff syllables of comfort and reproof
he feels himself lifted and, half-turning in his
Grandfather's clasp, feels the old heart beating
against his hand, and himself, a little dazed . . .

held aloft between two.

FACTS ABOUT SOME SEQUOIA COMPANIONS

Spotted Bat

Black, with large and easily recognizable white spots, the spotted bat belongs to the unique order of bats, the *chiroptera*, which are unrelated to rodents. Roosting in the crevices, and feeding mostly on moths, it is one of the few bats that uses echolocation frequencies low enough to be audible to humans. It is thought that this is a tactic used to catch moths. As many moth species have evolved tympanic membranes that are specifically tuned to the very high frequencies emitted by most bat species, the lower frequency used by the spotted bat cannot be heard by the moths.

A striking animal, it has pink wings and matching translucent pink ears, nearly as long as its body. At about four inches, the ears are the largest of any bat in North America. They are held direct and forward during flight, but curled up to conserve heat and water when the bat roosts.

In spite of the fourteen-inch wingspan, it is a delicate creature, weighing only about three-quarters of an ounce. A newborn is one quarter of that—about the size of a grape.

Many temperate zone bat species have evolved to delay fertilization over their time of hibernation. Sperm is sequestered so that it doesn't meet the egg until spring, in order that the bat pup will be weaned by the time insect activity is peaking.[23]

Common Camas

Also called wild hyacinth, or *Quamash*, it was once considered part of the Lily family, but with advanced DNA and biochemical studies, the camas have been placed in the Agave family. *Camas* is a Nootka Indian word meaning "sweet." These plants, once found in enormous numbers, were an important staple food for American Indian tribes. When steamed, one-third of the bulb's weight is fructose, and they were eaten like sweet potatoes, or dried and made into a meal. Wars were fought over access to their supply.

California Patch Butterfly

Like many other species of insects, the California patch employs a peculiar method of locating mates described as "hilltopping." The males perch and patrol a ridge top, sometimes for several days, mating

< 120 >

< Secret Voices from the Forest >

with females who arrive with the same purpose. Assumedly, the male at the very top will have shown himself the most fit for breeding. Studies have shown that even slight elevation differences on flat terrain can trigger this behavior.[24]

Snowbank Orangepeel Fungus

The *Caloscypha fulgens* is distinguishable for its bright, yellow-orange cups, which discolor bluish-green with age.

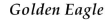

This fungus parasitizes conifer seeds. As with many of the *Ascomycetes* type of fungus, the sac in which the spores develop is under pressure. So when disturbed, it will quickly blow out the spores in a visible cloud above the cup.[25]

Golden Eagle

One of North America's largest predatory birds, the Golden Eagle is most common in the West. Once widespread across most of the Northern Hemisphere, it has acquired a prominent place in human lore and culture.

Because of their speed and agility, Golden Eagles have been used in falconry for centuries, and due to their size and natural tendency of mates to hunt in pairs, were used in teams to hunt larger animals, such as deer and wolves.

The Golden Eagle is the national bird of five nations, and has been used as the coat of arms for at least ten countries. It was the model for the *aquila*, the standard of the Roman legions.

Sacred to many North American Indians throughout the continent, the feathers of the Golden Eagle often hold a most sacred place in their religious ceremonies, and are used to honor bravery and good leadership. This bird is also thought to be the model for the legendary Thunderbird.

Pairs of Golden Eagles usually mate for life, and have a long nesting season so their young have time to reach independence. Their territory is large, containing up to fourteen huge high nests, and covering an area of twenty to sixty square miles. The number of young depends on the weather and the size of the rabbit population, which is their main prey, although they are capable of killing much larger animals.[26]

Western Moss Heather

This small, ground-hugging shrub native to subalpine areas of western North America is used in floral arrangements, and traditionally signifies protection and the fulfillment of wishes made. It is not the same plant as the famous heather of the Scottish moors, but is also a member of the Heath family. Some believe that the genus name, *cassiope mertensiana*, was inspired by the star-shaped flowers to commemorate Cassiopeia, who lives forever among the stars as a constellation.

Yosemite Toad

This reptile lives only in the high Sierras, in damp meadows and forest margins, near permanent sources of water. Like many toads, it is slow moving—usually walking or crawling. For self-defense, it relies on its parotid glands, located behind the eyes, which secrete a toxin that can inflame the mouth and throat of a would-be predator.

< 122 >

Canyon Dudleya

This is a brightly colored member of a family commonly called "Stone-crop," as they are found on sunny rocks, or rocky slopes. The canyon dudleya is also called "Live Forever," from the Maidu tribe, who saw them growing out of rock. It is from a long-lived group of plants, some reputedly as old as one hundred years. When cultivating this species, it is essential to *avoid* summer watering![27]

Mountain Lion

With the exception of humans, the mountain lion has the largest range of any mammal in the Western Hemisphere. It once ranged from the Yukon to the coastal mountains of Tierra del Fuego and from east to west, across the entire continent of North America. It occupied more territory and more environmental niches than any other land mammal, other than man, in the Western Hemisphere. Although greatly reduced in numbers since European colonization, it has still managed to retain much of its original distribution.

< Secret Voices from the Forest >

The mountain lion holds the Guinness record for the animals with the highest number of names. In the English language, the mountain lion has more than forty names, among them cougar or puma.

Unlike the tiger or the African lion, the mountain lion cannot roar because of the structure of its larynx, or voice box. Instead, it produces a high-pitched scream.[28]

Monument Plant

This is a *monocarpic* plant, which, after growing for many years, flowers once and then dies. The monument plant has a lifespan of twenty to eighty years and can reach heights of over six feet. The flower emerges from a large basal rosette of leaves. It is common to find many plants grouped together on a sunny open hillside, within a small area. Large numbers periodically flower all at once, every two to four years, apparently as a result of a wet summer the previous year.

< 123 >

Sierra Nevada Ensatina

Breathing through its skin, this lungless salamander does not have an aquatic larval stage, but instead hatches as a miniature adult. Living as long as fifteen years, this amphibian requires a damp environment in which to move, hunt, and breed.

Although the ensatina is the most widely distributed lungless salamander in the West, found from British Columbia through the Baja peninsula, several subspecies, called *Ensatina eschscholtzi*, form a ring around the mountains of the California Central Valley. The Sierra Nevada ensatina exists only in these mountains.

In what is thought to be a classic example of Darwinian evolution by gradualism, DNA studies supports the idea that *Ensatina eschscholtzi* is a species *complex* that is now breaking up; it is an accumulation of micro-mutations that is now leading to the formation of new species.[29]

< Pacific Coast Ranges and the Great Basin : Sequoia >

NATURE AS MUSE

The Greeks considered the Muses to be an aspect of the Great Goddess, and the source of inspiration for creative ideas. Poetry, literature, music and the arts are ways by which the unknowable wisdom of Spirit is transmitted into a form comprehensible to the rest of us.

In his historical study of poetic inspiration, *The White Goddess*, Robert Graves theorized, "the function of poetry is religious invocation of the Muse." He also felt that the Muse was there to remind man that "he must keep in harmony with the family of living creatures among which he was born, by obedience to the lady of the house."

Earth itself is the Goddess and the Muse. The Muse inspires the poet, the writer, the artist, and the musician to communicate that which cannot be spoken, and to teach us how to offer respect by being *as* She is—a lover of life and of the creation itself.

Living on this planet is not easy. It is in a state of constant change, a great deal of it violent and unexpected. That very violence has taught all creatures to be in awe and fear of Earth's immense power. We, as humans, have spent most of our existence finding ways to not only survive from day to day, but to protect ourselves from the unexpected—the hurricane, the tornado, the earthquake and the tsunami, and the countless other means by which our fragile bodies can be destroyed as easily as a leaf falls from a tree.

But is this any different from what Earth itself faces? The very creative processes of our planet, of our solar system, of the countless suns and stars in the universe were, and continue to be, the vehicle of forces of incalculable might. At any time, a passing asteroid or comet, the solar wind, or the explosion of another celestial body could extinguish all that this planet has become in one terrifying instant.

Daily struggle is not only the fate of all who dwell here, but a reflection of the nature of the universe, and as such, the mystery of existence itself. How could such astonishing beauty, in so many forms, be the product of such destructive forces? Creation and destruction—two sides of the dualistic nature of reality—all one, but as one moves from the center, the one becomes two, in opposition.

We have been faced with this dilemma for as long as we have had time to consider philosophy, as well as survival. Perhaps the simplest idea is the best. Live, but not in fear.

Many, believing that there is life on other planets, dream of traveling to the far reaches of Space. One of the most striking visual images to come from our first venture off the planet's surface is that of the Earth as seen from the surface of our Moon. Our bright jewel of blue and green, with its swirling clouds and atmosphere, is completely unlike anything that we have been able to see with our most powerful telescopes. Even if we are someday able to travel far enough to discover life elsewhere, nothing we find may ever be of as great beauty and value as this Earth—our Mother Earth.

≫≫≫≫≫≫≫≫≫≫≫≫≫≫≫≫≫≫≫≫≫≫≫≫≫≫≫≫≫≫≫≫≫≫≫

CHAPTER FOUR

THE ROCKY MOUNTAINS

in the cold mountain air
a golden eagle
sailing the coral dawn

>=>=>=>=>=>=>=<=<=<=<=<=<=<

THE ROCKY MOUNTAINS:
COLUMBIA, COLORADO, AND WASATCH
TEMPERATE CONIFEROUS FORESTS

The Rocky Mountains extend more than three thousand miles, from New Mexico through western Canada into Alaska, between the Great Plains on the east and a series of broad basins and plateaus on the west.

The Rockies are also distinguished by the Continental Divide, which winds its way through the mountains, separating rivers that flow either to the Pacific or the Atlantic Ocean. Runoff and snowmelt from the peaks feed Rocky Mountain rivers and lakes with the water that supplies one-quarter of the United States.

The Rockies were formed by several factors—movement of tectonic plates, and resulting volcanic activity, which injected great masses of molten rock horizontally. After this hardened in place, further movement of plates and volcanic activity caused uplift, and erosion from water and glaciers did the rest. Apparently, the Rockies are still getting higher!

The Theory of Plate Tectonics postulates that Earth's outer layer is made up of plates, which have moved throughout Earth's history. It is believed that 225 million years ago, there was one giant supercontinent, called *Pangaea*. It began to split apart around 200 million years ago. The separate plates spread apart and oceans filled the spaces between. The plates continue to move at the rate of about a quarter inch a year.

It has been shown that Pangaea was not the first supercontinent, only the most recent. There were several others before Pangaea. There is geological and fossil evidence showing that the breaking up and formation of supercontinents appears to be a cycle that has been occurring throughout Earth's 4.6 billion year history.[1]

When one plate meets another, there are various possible outcomes. Because the rock of a land mass is of lesser density, it will be more buoyant, so an oceanic plate pushing toward a land mass will always slide underneath. However, when two continental plates meet, neither will slide under the other. Instead, the two crush together at what is known as a collisional boundary. They crumple and fold, some pieces of land thrusting over or under other pieces, resulting in a mountain range.[2]

The Rocky Mountains are a relatively young system that formed on top of a much more ancient mountain range. These older mountains were likely formed during the collision of earlier plate formations, and worn down by erosion.

< 128 >

< Secret Voices from the Forest >

Beginning roughly 170 million years ago, the Pacific plate, moving north, collided with the North American plate as it moved west. Because the oceanic plate slid underneath the continental plate at a shallow angle, it lifted up the more ancient mountains. During a repeating cycle of major mountain-building episodes, with interim periods in which stress was built up, the Rocky Mountains were raised. This process ended around forty million years ago.

Since then, erosion by water and glaciers has sculpted the mountain range into dramatic valleys and peaks. At the end of the last ice age, about eleven thousand years ago, humans started to inhabit the mountain range.

Prehistoric humans developed a subsistence way of life, based on elevation and seasons. From late spring to mid-summer, people occupied the lower elevations. They waited for the snow to recede, following the migration of elk, bighorn sheep, bison and deer back up to the heights. Hunters returned to the same areas each year, and there is evidence that they used game drives, constructing ambush blinds and narrow corridors, taking advantage of natural confining terrain to trap large numbers of animals at once.

In spite of the long seasons of harsh conditions, there was plentiful game and wild plant species to allow for maintenance of these bands of early hunter-gatherers.[3]

The Rocky Mountains are composed of over forty distinct mountain ranges, each with unique ecological features, so there is no one ecosystem for the entire region. Ecologists divide the Rocky Mountains into a number of zones, each defined by its physical characteristics—altitude, mean temperature, amount and type of precipitation—or if it contains mountains, deserts, or bodies of water, as well as the plants and animals it supports. Each zone is further defined by whether or not it can support trees, and the presence of one or more *indicator species*, also known as a *bioindicator*, which is a species of plant or animal that is more susceptible to environmental change, and therefore their presence, absence, or general health can be used to gather information about a certain environment. Lichen and frogs are both indicator species.[4]

The Rocky Mountains are an important habitat for a great deal of well-known wildlife, such as elk, moose, mule and white-tailed deer, pronghorns, mountain goats, bighorn sheep, black bears, grizzly bears, coyotes, lynxes, and wolverines. North America's largest herd of moose is in the Alberta-British Columbia foothills forests.[5]

≼ QUAKING ASPEN ≽

REFLECTIONS on THE UNCOUNTABLE NUMBER, THE INEXHAUSTABLE SUPPLY

What Aspen Can Tell You About Itself

We are rooted in the soul of the Earth, which never dies. We are being called to grow and multiply—to rise to the surface in consciousness. All creatures are becoming aware of a source that is more than a collection of forms.

Family is important. It is the sum total of the previous generation—reincarnation, if you like. There is a sense of the underground connection of the clone, which has a subterranean feel—a dark, churning sense. We were once *part* of the soil, moving, grinding up to form smaller particles. There is no such thing as an inanimate object, as everything has directional intent, or the desire to change itself into something else.

It is important to identify with the One-Big-Thing-that-is-Many-Things, and a sense of purposeful unity, much like being in an army—mindless, or unconsciously directed. Isn't that how we all are, on some level—our movement dictated by outside forces, be they weather or the urge to live?

We love the color white. It makes us stand out in comparison to others, and against our surroundings. This is not self-conceit; it is merely one of the infinite variations that has occurred as the physical manifests and divides. Being near the mountains gives us the chance to see more whiteness—it makes the world seem bigger.

We have learned that comfort is necessary for all things from time to time, on a planet of violence and uncertainty. The planet itself provides these means of respite, since it is the source of the violent changes. It understands the need.

Aspen's Place in the World

Aspen sees life as a dream, as there are massive forces beneath the surface reality that are the source of motion and change.

Its place in the world is to be a reflection of these forces. Superficially, the first thing that is noticeable is an inconsequential chattering and preoccupation with the mundane, manifest in the "quaking" of its literally billions of leaves. Beneath is the gradual, tenacious acquisition of territory. It doesn't believe the world will end, as long as there is even the tiniest spark of this force in existence.

The Willow Family is the essence of "group-consciousness," which thinks as a great multitude, but works as a unit—in placement, in the means by which offspring is scattered, and in the way connection is made through roots. Having a reality along the lines of "bigger is better," they become more capable of surviving in a *big* world. This particular species, Quaking Aspen, maintains a balance between youth and age. The collective age of its root system is great and has vast accumulated knowledge. It also maintains a perspective of eternal youth by keeping the part of itself that is above ground of short experience, supple youth, and infinite new growth.

Aspen's Message for Us

Humanity brings a carnival spirit, a sense of surprise, competition and pageantry to the day-to-day concerns of living. Like us, they spread their seed far and wide, are forced to move with the ebb and flow of the planet's geological forces, and wish to hold on to a physical form. But unlike the rest of us, they struggle against Death. In that way they are like the geological forces—unpredictable, ungovernable—creating the chaos that leads to the creation of new forms.

The Law of Survival has always dictated that creatures be driven by an imperative to multiply in physical number, but this is beginning to change. Balance has become disturbed, and *will* be restored. The process often involves violence, but will not come as a result of judgment, or an assessment of blame.

< 132 >

Keeping one's promise, in perpetuity, is relative to the duration of life. It is appealing to believe that one's *own* sense of the eternal is the ultimate definition, but this is a term that applies respectively to trees and humans alike, as it would an ant or a cloud. All things have their allotted time, and perpetuity is relative to this certainty.

Humans tend to see themselves as separate from or outside of creation—different. This is not the case. The human species, although consisting of individuals, has a *group* function as well. As all things have their purpose in the creative and destructive cycles of the universe, so does the human race. Coming to an understanding of this would remove some of the conflict in their minds.

We have said that our collective being is rooted in the soul of the Earth, which never dies. For those who care selflessly for the Earth and its creatures, by manifesting this quality they are learning to work *with*, or *enhance* natural processes.

To progress further, learn to believe in possibilities. *Become* balance.

< Secret Voices from the Forest >

CHRONICLES

These are the most widely dispersed trees on the continent, and the second most in the world. Quaking aspens are found throughout all the Canadian provinces, all but thirteen southeastern states in the U.S., and the higher altitudes in Mexico. Their range to the north is limited by intolerance of permafrost, and to the south by a dislike of hot summers.

Quaking aspen is a member of the large Willow family, whose members, numbering around 350 different species, include not only the many kinds of willow, but also cottonwoods, poplars and aspens. In the East, aspens are only a small part of the predominant hardwood tree species, but in the West they are some of the few that can survive the arid climate.

This is partially due to their massive root systems, which can expand almost infinitely. The roots of a single tree can spread nearly one hundred feet laterally, and extend ten feet deep. They depend on periodic fire and other disturbances to maintain their numbers. When other trees have burned, space is cleared that allows sunlight, which the aspen requires — it is extremely intolerant of shade.

Although it quite often provides protective shelter for young conifers and other slower-growing trees, quaking aspen will die out when its charges grow taller and begin to overshadow it.

Quaking aspens have adapted well to fire. Although their thin, green bark has little resistance, so much moisture is maintained in the trees that an extensive aspen grove has been known to make a hot, crowning fire drop down to the ground, allowing containment. Even if all the above-ground stems are killed, the root system will usually be left undamaged, and immediately

< 133 >

< The Rocky Mountains : Temperate Coniferous Forests : Quaking Aspen >

afterwards will send up numerous fast-growing shoots that will out-compete most other forms of vegetation.

While the lifespan of an individual tree in the colony is relatively short—only 150 years in the West—a continuous colony of aspens can be an extremely long-lived organism. A colony is considered a single organism, and the largest known one of these, named Pando (Latin for "I spread"), is near Fishlake, Utah. It is estimated by some to be eighty thousand years old, stretches over more than one hundred acres, weighs in excess of thirteen million pounds, and includes some 47,000 individual tree stems.

The quaking aspen is adaptable, able to thrive in many types of soil, but prefers cool, dry summers, and winters with a lot of snow. It does not do well in permanently wet soils, although it is considered a riparian species—one that tends to locate near wetlands.

Although it produces millions of fluffy white seeds, its usual method of propagation in the West is through vegetative sprouts growing from the roots, or *cloning*. As a result, an aspen tends to grow in colonies, and all the trees in any one colony have identical characteristics and share a single root system. A mature root system can put out 400,000 to one million shoots per acre, and the sprouts can grow a meter per growing season.

Propagation by seed is also limited by the fact that an aspen is either male or female, and a large stand is usually all clones of the same sex. Even if pollinated, the small seeds (three million per pound) are only able to germinate for a short time, as they lack a stored food source or a protective coating.

Stands of quaking aspen are as important to wildlife as habitat in the dry western States. Shrubs and grasses are thicker under aspen stands than that of the canopy of a group of conifers. Unlike many other trees, their white outer bark is capable of photosynthesis, and is as nutritious as other kinds of vegetation. Since aspen does not have to be dug out of the snow, deer and elk eat the bark over the winter. A favorite food for beavers, they often use aspen stems as the main structural elements for their dams.

Due to the structure of its flexible, flattened leaf stalk, called a *petiole*, the leaves of the

< 134 >

< Secret Voices from the Forest >

quaking aspen flutter even in the slightest breeze. This gives the leaves both strength and flexibility, and may help the tree survive storms, as the clumping action of the leaves reduces resistance to wind.

A promising technology that is being used to clean up environmental contaminants from soil, air, or water is called phytoremediation—the use of plants to reduce or eliminate pollutants without needing to contain, excavate, or completely remove contaminated material from the problem area. This works because plants change toxic chemicals into less harmful chemicals within themselves. Or they can change them into gases, via transpiration. Plants put down roots into the soil to draw water and nutrients up into the stems and leaves. Some of this water is returned to the air by transpiration.

Studies have revealed that about 10 percent of the moisture found in the atmosphere is released by plants through transpiration. The remaining 90 percent is mainly supplied by evaporation from oceans, seas, and other bodies of water, such as lakes, rivers, or streams.[6]

During transpiration, the harmful chemicals are reduced to harmless trace amounts when combined with the air. Organic solvents, PCBs, heavy metals, *polyaromatic hydrocarbons* (potent atmospheric pollutants, many of which are carcinogenic), explosives, oils, pesticides and chemical fertilizers can be removed by various grasses, water plants, algae, and trees whose roots have a strong pumping ability, like willows, poplars, and aspen.

This knowledge, which has up to now been employed to clean up large areas of industrial or chemical pollution, can also be applied to yards and home gardens. Down-to-earth, problem-specific information is available which plants to use to clean up many different types of pollutant.[7]

QUAKING ASPEN COMPANIONS

Elf Butterfly
Red Osier Dogwood
Buffalo Gourd
Yellow-bellied Marmot

Wheel Milkweed
Greenwinged Teal
Shrubby Willow Herb
Great Basin Spadefoot Toad
Western Coralbean

Clustered Lady's Slipper
Blue Mud Dauber
Cutthroat Trout
Golden Coral Fungus

Grey Wolf
Vase Flower
Evening Grosbeak
Colorado Blue Spruce
Western Fence Lizard

In the rustling of an aspen's leaves
    can be heard the quiet clamor
of uncountable spirits tapping and scraping
at the windows of form;
a *sotto voce* seething
of the urge to be,
whether of seeds or souls,
cluttering the wind.

But why listen
to the mad signaling of desire?
Why should we listen? We are trees,
with limbs of knotty ligamental strakes,
bark that bleeds green at the bite of an axe,
and flowers lacing the high air
with invisible scents.
What have we to do
with the hunger of ghosts?

Yet all through the day the fractious chatter
never completely dies; even at night
these pallid leaves quiver and sigh
with love for the wind-borne
moon.

FACTS ABOUT SOME QUAKING ASPEN COMPANIONS

Western Fence Lizard

In 1998, researchers reported that an unidentified protein in the blood of the common western fence lizard could eventually be the basis of a treatment for Lyme disease. It has been found that immature black-legged ticks, feeding on the blood of the western fence lizard, are purified of any Lyme bacterium they may be carrying in the their guts. "We've speculated on this for years, and now we have fairly good evidence that this is the case . . . lizards are doing humanity a great service here," said Robert Lane, a University of California at Berkeley insect biologist who has been studying ticks and Lyme disease for more than a decade.

First identified in 1975, Lyme disease is the most common tick-borne disease in the Northern Hemisphere. If left untreated, it affects the joints, heart, and central nervous system.[8]

< 138 >

Red-osier Dogwood

A widespread shrub in North America, its showiness is due to its bright reddish-purple twigs, long used for basket weaving. A blended smoking mixture called *kinnikinnick* was made by a number of American Indian tribes from the shrub's inner bark.

It is capable of tolerating extremely cold temperatures—in laboratory experiments, down to -320°F. Acclimation to extreme cold is thought to have developed in response to Ice Age conditions—short days, water stress, and long twilights at high altitudes, where far red light is a characteristic factor.

Far red light is light at the extreme red end of the visible spectrum, between red and infrared light. Although it is only dimly visible to human eyes, it is "perceived" by a leaf pigment, called a *phytochrome*—a pigment responding to light. The plant uses it to regulate the time of flowering, based on the length of day and night. It also regulates the germination of seeds, leaf-characteristics, and the absorbance of cholophyll.[9]

< Secret Voices from the Forest >

Yellow-bellied Marmot

About the size of a house cat, the yellow-bellied marmot is one of fourteen recognized species of marmots, which are large ground squirrels. Woodchucks and groundhogs are also marmots, and they are the only animal after which a U.S. holiday is named. At least three woodchucks predict the weather on Groundhog Day: Punxsutawney Phil, Beauregard Lee, and Wiarton Willie. Phil has been in the business since 1887, but according to the *Stormfax Almanac*, the groundhog's seasonal forecasting accuracy is somewhat low. Phil's winter prognostications have been correct only 39 percent of the time.[10]

Groundhog Day is an outgrowth of Candlemas Day, a tradition brought to Pennsylvania from Germany in the 1700s. The origins of Candlemas itself lie in the ancient pagan celebration of *Imbolc*, midway between the Winter Solstice and the Spring Equinox. This time was dreary and dark for the early inhabitants of northern Europe, yet the promise of spring and new life were already seen to be at work. The ewes began to lactate for the coming lambs, and it was known that hibernating animals awoke and gave birth at this time, so that their offspring would be sufficiently grown to survive when they emerged from their dens later. The tradition held that bright sun on that day forebode further winter weather, but clouds or storms meant that spring had taken hold for good.[11]

People who study woodchucks and other marmots are called "marmoteers" or "marmotologists." These biologists may attend the International Conference of the Genus Marmota, held every three or four years, each time in a different city.

< 139 >

Wheel Milkweed

There are over one hundred species of milkweed in North America, which is a host plant for the larva of the monarch butterfly. Its leaves contain a compound called a *cardiac glycoside*, which is a toxin that makes the caterpillar noxious to predators. Humans have historically used this compound as either a tonic or a poison.

Today it is widely used in the modern treatment of congestive heart failure and for the treatment of atrial fibrillation and flutter. On a non-medicinal note, planting milkweed in a garden will draw not only Monarchs, but many other butterfly species, as well as honeybees and hummingbirds. There are many varieties of milkweed, and seeds are available for purchase.[12]

< The Rocky Mountains : Temperate Coniferous Forests : Quaking Aspen >

Grey Wolf

The wolf is the largest member of the canine family, and the ancestor of the domestic dog. It has been long assumed that Mesolithic man, about fifteen to seventeen thousand years ago, tamed the wolf and began selective breeding that resulted in the dog. However, a fascinating new theory has surfaced — that the wolf tamed itself!

This hypothesis asserts that smaller, lower-ranked wolf pack members, who were less aggressive than the pack leaders, and only allowed access to a kill after the others had eaten their fill, might have found human refuse dumps a more reliable source of food. These wolves, by nature less fearful of humans, were more likely to survive and produce offspring.

It has been found in studies of silver foxes that lack of fear is not the product of training, but of genetics, which passes to the offspring. This study, carried out by Russian researcher Dmitry Belyaev from 1959 through the mid-1980s, also showed that other recessive traits accompanied domestication — physical changes, such as floppy ears, curly or shorter tails, less fear, unusual color variations in fur, and barking.[13]

< 140 >

Buffalo Gourd

This member of the Squash family has a huge perennial taproot — sometimes eighteen inches across at ground level, extending three feet deep, with a shape something like a big carrot — that produces annual fruit-bearing vines that can grow as long as 650 feet. It is grows rapidly and adapts well to dry climates and disturbed soils.

American Indian tribes have used all parts of the buffalo gourd for thousands of years, to make ritual rattles and kitchen utensils, soap and cosmetics, medicines and food. The plant was considered by some tribes to have special healing powers. They believed that the shape taken by the root would dictate the condition on the body in need of treatment.

The seeds, high in protein and fat content, are edible, and were roasted or boiled and sometimes ground into a meal. But they are the only part of the plant that can be consumed by humans or sheep and cattle. They, like all wild gourds, contain chemicals called *cucurbitacins*, which are bitter tasting and somewhat toxic. The buffalo gourd contains a very

< Secret Voices from the Forest >

high level of these chemicals, which produces a particularly foul odor responsible for another common name, "stink gourd." Its scientific name is *Cucurbita foetidissima*, "most fetid."

But in the category of "a rose by any other name," this plant, unpleasant smelling to us, is irresistible to corn rootworms and cucumber beetles. Farmers use this attraction to their advantage by planting buffalo gourd alongside their squash, cucumbers, melons and corn, drawing the insects away from valuable food crops, and reducing the need for chemical pesticides.[14]

Cutthroat Trout

Native to western North America, cutthroat trout are the most diverse and widely dispersed stream-dwelling trout in the Western Hemisphere. Because their habitat is generally rugged, populations become isolated, each native to a different drainage basin. As a result, there are now fourteen recognized subspecies. Various species are the State Fish of Idaho, Wyoming, Colorado, Montana, Nevada, New Mexico, and Utah.

Although they vary in basic coloration from grey to green, all populations have distinctive red, pink, or orange marks on the underside of the jaw or gill plates. The common name "cutthroat" refers to these markings.

Clustered Lady's Slipper

A native North American orchid, the clustered lady's slipper is also known as the American valerian, because early settlers found that its extract was a good substitute for the valerian they had used as a sedative in Europe. They were directed to this flower by the Indian tribes, who had long used it for calming the nerves. Because of loss of habitat, this flower has become rare and expensive to use as an herbal medicine, and is protected by the U.S. Forest Service in all National Forests where it occurs.

Its seeds are unique, as they are underdeveloped when mature, remaining dormant until invaded by soil fungi. The seedling then enlarges and becomes bulb-like, at which point it is capable of photosynthesis and growth. The process takes up to three years, during which time the plant is completely subterranean and dependent on the fungi to supply it with all water and nutrients.[15]

REFLECTIONS ON ETERNAL YOUTH

What Bristlecone Can Tell You About Itself

*E*ternal Youth to me means always keeping a fresh perspective. My past simply recedes, sloughs away behind the forward movement of new growth. I believe that each day brings new possibilities. This day will be different from the day before, so we cannot imagine how things will turn out.

I recognize this same quality in everything around me: in the air, made up of constantly moving particles of light and energy that react unpredictably to greater forces, influencing the planet from outside its atmosphere; in the animals, busily doing what is necessary to survive; in the soil and the mountains, grinding slowly into new forms that will create new conditions. All things create change, as well as give response.

I am drawn to the mountains. Not only do they look out onto the world, but they also transmit a sense of personal independence. I was once part of the body of the mountains, but I didn't want to remain gravel—it was too broken and separate. So I became something that was attached, with roots going into the mountain itself. Attachment can be a good thing, if gifts are shared.

While I am pleased simply to be in existence, I do enjoy creating a few little things that add interest or uniqueness to the mix—like the colors and shapes of my offspring, and the forms of truth taken by the Elders among us.

Bristlecone's Place in the World

I am one who brings memory into the present, and then nudges it into the future. I dream that I am able to merge with other solid objects, as if the physical dimension did not present any boundaries. In this way I can assimilate the nature of anything that presents itself to me. The planet also wishes to comprehend all, and accomplishes this by morphing—twisting, turning and grinding into a variety of platforms upon which the greater play can be acted out.

I come from a large extended family—the Pines—but the subspecies to which I belong tends to be picky in its choices of where to grow. As a result, I sometimes find myself isolated, because in accommodating the conditions of the elements in my surroundings, I can outlast my neighbors. It has taught me to be tolerant, and take interest in others, whoever they are. There are whole worlds of activity going on underground—insects, microbes, and small burrowing animals. Their kingdoms begin, reach their zeniths, and then, when it looks like they are dying, they transform into something new.

The biggest change I have seen since my species came into being is less callousness about life and death. The growing disquiet that the planet feels about the dissolution of forms is translating itself into an elevation of consciousness. Life and death may still happen, but the division between them will seem more translucent as time goes on.

Bristlecone's Message for Us

In spite of the adage that "failing to remember the past will condemn one to repeat its mistakes," it is human nature to look ahead to the future. It would be a mistake to passively wait for the imposition of "fate," or to respond to the unpredictability of life by defending. Making choices based on optimism makes one a shaper of the future.

By embracing my concept of Eternal Youth, humanity could learn to have more certainty. They should not become mired in problems that are the result of a fearful outlook. The resulting anxiety will only bring stagnation, by squelching hope, possibility, wonder, and an appreciation of simply being here in the first place.

Age is relative, but when one lives long enough, it can be observed that the cycles of life renew themselves many times. Each time will appear different from the last.

Never believe that you will only become what your genes predict.

< 144 >

An element of humanity has come forward in this incarnation to take on the role of The Destroyer. It is a brave act. Because of the mental conflict in which it is human nature to engage, and which this act engenders, these individuals will burden themselves with despair and self-condemnation.

The Destroyer is not evil. The task facing humanity is to be released from conflict — when that happens, the methods of performing this duty will alter.

Do not hide from your true natures, but remember that exposure does not guarantee knowledge of truth, or even self-acceptance. There is a fine line between looking, with happy anticipation, to the Future-Within-the-Present, and hiding your heads in the sand.

In the end, gratitude is the key to Eternal Youth.

< Secret Voices from the Forest >

CHRONICLES

When one refers to a bristlecone pine, the picture that comes to mind is that of a gnarled skeleton, streaks of color displayed in its twisted hulk, only strips of bark and a few sprigs of green life remaining. These particular trees are indeed ancient, and one species of Foxtail pine, the Great Basin bristlecone, has become famous as the world's oldest species of tree. The current known individual is nicknamed Methuselah—as of 2011, aged 4,843 years. Its exact location is kept secret, since an older specimen, nicknamed "Prometheus," was cut down in 1964.

The oldest trees are found in the Ancient Bristlecone Pine Forest of the White Mountains near Bishop, California. They stand on north-facing slopes, averaging two thousand years old, as compared to one thousand years for trees growing on the southern slopes. The dryness of the climate and the density and resin-content of their wood can preserve them long after death, with dead trees as old as seven thousand years standing next to live ones.

The bristlecone pine is so named for the bottlebrush appearance formed by the needles on their shoots and smaller limbs. There are three members in the small subspecies of the Pine family called the foxtail pines, which all occur exclusively in the western United States in the high mountains of California, Arizona, New Mexico, Colorado, Utah, and Nevada.

The other two species, foxtail and Rocky Mountain bristlecone, do not seem to reach quite such advance ages as the Great Basin bristlecone. However, a recently discovered Rocky Mountain bristlecone pine, at 2,435

< 145 >

< The Rocky Mountains : Temperate Coniferous Forests : Bristlecone Pine >

years, nearly doubles the age of the previously known eldest of this species, so who can say what may be as yet undiscovered.

However, these wonders of nature have a youth, and begin like any other pine tree, standing straight upright. When a bristlecone finds itself situated in an area that does not get blasted with cold, dry winds, and is rooted in soil that is nutrient-rich, it will continue to grow straight, although its life will be shorter than that of its brothers living on remote, wind-swept mountain ridges.

The needles of most pines are shed after only a few years, from two to five, but the bristlecone can retain its needles for up to forty-five years. It has also been noted that the needle-retention of many species of pine living in higher elevations will double or even triple as a result of location.

In the complicated world of species classification, the number of existing species of pines numbers between 220 and 250, depending on the source.

The Rocky Mountain bristlecone is named *Aristata*, which means "bearded," a reference to the long, hooked spines on its cone scales. The pollinated cone takes two years to develop. The first year, the cones are small and blue, darkening the second year. Requiring cross-pollination, they are located at the top of the tree, where they are likely to catch the most wind-born pollen from other trees. The male flowers cluster on the lower branches and are yellow or orange in color.

It takes the bristlecone pine two to five times as long as other pines to become mature enough to bear cones, but then it will continue to produce viable seeds and cones as long as it lives.

Reasons for the longevity of bristlecone pines fall into two categories:

First, they have genetically adapted to high elevations with cold, dry climates. They are unique in their ability to live and thrive in some of the most extreme mountain conditions known, and have many water-conserving features that contribute to this fact:

- In rocky terrain, their roots wrap tightly around boulders, where they are anchored, and they can find water in the cracks between the rocks.
- They employ "sectored architecture," or strip barking—water moves up from the roots only to sections of the trunk directly above, and any damaged bark dies back. A ten-inch strip of strip of bark can sustain a large crown.
- Trees exposed to a constant prevailing wind lean over, offering a diminished profile, called a *krummholz*.
- Because it is produced so slowly, the wood of the bristlecone is very dense and strong, with high resin content and narrow annual rings, so it retains moisture and repels insects.

- The tree's needle bunches close up or do not grow as long during drought conditions.

Second, specific factors in these climates discourage competition and enemies.

- A tree line marks the limits of where trees can grow; it is the transition from forest to alpine habitats. As the elevation increases, the sites become increasingly harsh. The bristlecone pine is one of a handful of trees that commonly forms tree lines in western North America.

- They can live on rocky, nutrient-poor soil, low in nitrogen and phosphorus and high in dolomite and alkaline content.

- Few competitive species can survive in these conditions, including most groundcover plants, so the bristlecone grows with a lot of space between trees. When one tree catches fire because of a lightning strike, for instance, it doesn't spread to the surrounding trees.

- A mean annual temperature of 35°, with a growing season of less than four months was recorded for some Rocky Mountain bristlecone pine stands in New Mexico. The bark beetle breeds fewer generations in a short growing season.

Studies of ancient bristlecones have found no signs of degenerative aging. The trees continue to display living tissue and vital reproductive functions until some factor in their environment causes them to die—such as a lightning strike and resulting fire, exposure of the roots by erosion, or stripping of the bark by an animal.

The foxtail pines, like other nut-bearing pines, are an important food source for a variety of wildlife, including bears, squirrels and other rodents, as well as many birds. The Clark's Nutcracker forms a mutually beneficial relationship by helping disperse seed. It buries seeds an inch or more below ground, in caches, and those not retrieved have a chance to germinate and establish, protected from the elements.[16]

Professor Ronald M. Lanner, of Utah State University, has observed that most of the surviving bristlecones at higher elevations seem to have become established from nutcracker seed caches. The birds seem to be attracted to bristlecones because of their reliable seed production, compared to other pine species present in the same area. He believes that the bristlecone's success at high elevations is in fact largely due to the presence of the Clark's Nutcracker's seed caches, as wind-dispersed seeds on the dry summits can become too dehydrated to be viable.[17]

BRISTLECONE PINE COMPANIONS

Boletus Edulis Fungus
Common Alpine Butterfly
White-crowned Sparrow
Cushion Buckwheat

Wandering Garter Snake
Black Hawthorn
Northern Harrier
Arizona Fescue
Nine-spotted Ladybeetle

Tassel-eared Squirrel
Fringed Gentian
Rocky Mountain Maple
Painted Turtle

Case's Fitweed
Red-breasted Nuthatch
Canada Goldenrod
Grizzly Bear
Mountain Bluebell

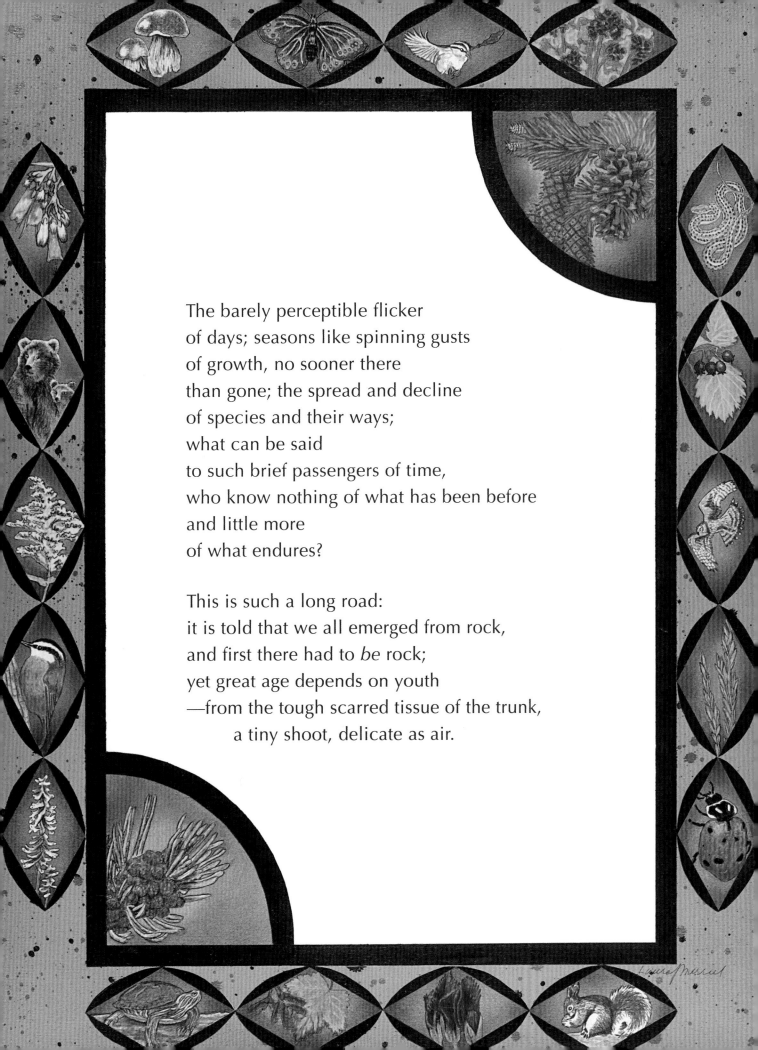

The barely perceptible flicker
of days; seasons like spinning gusts
of growth, no sooner there
than gone; the spread and decline
of species and their ways;
what can be said
to such brief passengers of time,
who know nothing of what has been before
and little more
of what endures?

This is such a long road:
it is told that we all emerged from rock,
and first there had to *be* rock;
yet great age depends on youth
—from the tough scarred tissue of the trunk,
    a tiny shoot, delicate as air.

FACTS ABOUT SOME BRISTLECONE PINE COMPANIONS

Grizzly Bear

The grizzly is also called the silvertip bear for its white-tipped fur. It is a subspecies of brown bear, whose ancestors originated in Eurasia. Living to an age of about twenty-five years in the wild, an adult male grizzly can stand as high as eight feet tall, and weigh over eight hundred pounds In spite of this bulk, it can move at an impressive speed of thirty miles per hour.

Although grizzlies have the digestive system of carnivores, favoring meat, plants make up 80 to 90 percent of their diet—much of that berries of various kinds. This is of mutual benefit to the fruit-bearing plants, as their seeds are dispersed, as well as fertilized, at the same time.

Grizzly bears are considered a keystone species in areas in which they range, as they control the populations of other animals that might otherwise overgraze the plant base.[18]

They have additional effects on their ecosystem through digging. While foraging for roots, bulbs, insects or small rodents, they will disturb the ground with their sizable claws, which increases availability of soil nitrogen and promotes a greater diversity of plants. The nitrogen is also increased through their habit of carrying salmon carcasses into the forest.

A bear, particularly a female, needs to gain as much as four hundred pounds before going into its den for the winter, so when it lives in an environment where salmon make spawning runs, this will be an important food source. Great gatherings of these normally solitary bears can be seen as the fish run upstream in huge numbers.

Although this species once ranged over most of North America, their numbers are greatly reduced. Today only about 1,000 grizzlies roam free in the continental U.S., and are protected by law, but in Alaska and western Canada, another 54,000 still remain.[19]

Boletus Edulis Fungus

This mushroom can be found in a symbiotic *ecto-mycorrhizal* association with conifers, particularly species of pine. This means there is an advantage for both

< 150 >

< Secret Voices from the Forest >

parties—the fungus aids the tree in absorbing nutrients, and in return receives sugars from the tree's photosynthesis.

In addition, *Boletus edulis* produces a number of organic compounds: a steroid derivative, various antioxidants and antiviral compounds, and one that gives the fungus resistance to toxic heavy metals.

White-crowned Sparrow

The White-crowned Sparrow has a small, pale pink or yellow bill, a long tail, and bold, easily recognizable black-and-white stripes on its head.

Like many North American songbirds, it migrates. It has been observed that this bird can stay awake for up to two weeks, even flying at night, without any reduction in alertness or physical ability. This is a mechanism that only functions during seasonal migration.

Black Hawthorn

Known by many names, including western thorn apple, the hawthorn's species name, *crataegus*, is from the Greek word "*kratos*," meaning "strength," referring to the hawthorn's strong wood. American Indian tribes used it for digging sticks and tool handles, and the common name, hawthorn, comes from its early use by the Anglo-Saxons as a hedge. Their word *haw* meant "hedge," and *haegthorn* meant "a fence with thorns."[20]

Because of their many long, sharp thorns, the hawthorn can form an impenetrable thicket that birds and small animals use for nesting and protection. The flowers draw many butterflies and other nectar-feeding insects and the berry-like fruit is an important source of winter food for many birds.

Wandering Garter Snake

The most common reptile in Yellowstone National Park, the garter snake is widespread throughout the continent. Due to its adaptability to climate and terrain, and lack of fussiness as to diet, it is the single most widely distributed genus of reptile in North America.

Western species are more dependent on water than those in the East. In the West, the wandering garter snake is less so, and tends to travel further away from water than other species of garter snake. It has been named "wandering" for that reason.

In some areas, wandering garter snakes overwinter in large groups. During hibernation, garter snakes typically occupy large, communal sites called *hibernacula*, emerging en masse in spring.[21]

Arizona Fescue

This is a perennial bunchgrass that lives for up to twenty years in ideal circumstances. It has a dense, fibrous root system that pushes deep, allowing it to tolerate dry conditions and trampling from grazing animals. It occurs in many environments, but is often found in open canopied coniferous forests, where it is an important source of food for elk in the summer.

It was discovered that the Arizona fescue's symbiotic relationship with the *Neotyphodium starrii* fungi gives it an increased resistance to seasonal drought and fires that frequent the Southwest.[22]

< 152 >

Red-breasted Nuthatch

The name "Nuthatch" refers to the bird's habit of using a crack as a tool, by wedging large seeds or insects inside, then hacking at it with their long, solid bills.

This bouncy, active bird breeds and lives in coniferous forests, excavating its nest in dead wood. Forming monogamous pairs, both sexes coat the inside and outside of the nest hole entrance with pitch to keep predators and competitors away. It avoids the pitch by flying straight into the hole.

Using strong legs and claws to move up, down, and sideways—sometimes descending head first—it searches for hidden insects in furrows and crevices.[23]

Canada Goldenrod

A perennial occurring throughout North America, the Goldenrod is often unfairly blamed for causing hay fever in humans. The pollen causing

< Secret Voices from the Forest >

these allergy problems is mainly produced by Ragweed—which blooms at the same time as the goldenrod, but is wind-pollinated. Goldenrod pollen is too heavy and sticky to be blown far from the flowers, and is thus mainly pollinated by insects.[24]

Painted Turtle

Its ancestors extending back fifteen million years, this widespread pond turtle lives in slow-moving, fresh water habitat, such as ponds, lakes, marshes, and creeks. It spends its days basking in the sun to maintain body temperature, eliminate parasites, and synthesize vitamin D3. When the turtle needs to sleep, it does so underwater, buried in the sand or mud at the bottom of the stream or pond. The Painted turtle has the ability to absorb oxygen from water, and so can remain submerged.

Turtles have no vocal cords, although they sometimes hiss, and no teeth, so they prefer to swallow their food whole. Their sex is not a process of genetics, but environment. Sex is determined by external temperature during the development of an embryo while inside the egg casing. Colder temperatures produce males and hotter ones make females.

They can live to be forty years old. When they grow, their shells expand in area by shedding the outer layer on thirteen separate bone plates. The new layer grows in larger, and also has a ring around its edge that, like the rings in the cross-section of a tree, will tell you the turtle's age.[25]

Rocky Mountain Maple

A small, delicate tree or shrub, it is the northernmost maple in North America, and many grazing animals, both wild and domestic, enjoy its leaves and tender shoots. It is a beautifully colored tree most of the year, with pairs of winged, reddish "keys," or seeds, and red leaves in the fall.

< 153 >

< The Rocky Mountains : Temperate Coniferous Forests : Bristlecone Pine >

❧ OAK/SERVICEBERRY ❧

REFLECTIONS ON LOVE

What Oak and Serviceberry Can Tell You About Themselves

We believe that to *Love* is to provide comfort and safety, and a platform from which The Loved One can grow and thrive. It is also a manifestation of bravery, both because it allows others a way to expand and realize their own natures, and for us, because the act of expressing love exposes us to the possibility of being completely consumed.

Although spring is our favorite season, when every creature and plant begins fresh, becoming the personification of optimism, we also need the cold and snowy winter. It is a time of rest, when we reconnect, and return to the earth to rejuvenate. Then we can see life as small animals do—those who depend on the bounty we produce to feed their young and live through the winter. We need to continually replenish our link with them, because by distributing our seeds, they play a great part in our reproduction.

We think about transformation, not simply in the manner that the flower becomes a fruit, but in the way that a seed is the representation of how the obliteration of death contains within it the promise of renewal.

We dream about relating—becoming the other, sometimes abandoning a consciousness of our original form, but without fear of losing anything truly important. It is as if a new world is being revealed.

Gambel Oak's and Western Serviceberry's Place in the World

We are evidence that beauty, sustenance and shelter will be available to any and all who have need, without discrimination. We have a symbiotic relationship with birds and other animals, allowing for greater diversity in more ways than simply the physical. There are so many to be fed, and each of us has a niche to fill. Our two species keep our crowns near to the ground, in order to make ourselves accessible.

The Earth is covered with a bountiful garden in which each element nourishes another, or it would not be present. The very nature of the planet is to nourish Life, and this is a quality . . . no, a mandate . . . that cannot be suppressed or inverted by fear.

Over its long history, Earth has become what it is now through trial and error. The process continues, and will do so into the future—no one knows the destination. She is thorough. Many approaches have been advanced, explored intensively, then sometimes abandoned or even reversed before something entirely new is ventured.

In the distant past, when we first began to take form, there were different plants and animals, and the landscape was different. But the weather will always be unpredictable, as the intensity of storms has sometimes weakened, and sometimes intensified. Gaia goes through times of simmering, pondering, feeling her way to the next step in her evolution. She's doing it again right now.

We are here to teach about renewal, not resignation or acceptance — rather, an embracing of change. To see oneself as a link in the chain can be a joyful way to live. We receive the raw materials of love from the body of the planet itself, becoming a conduit for Gaia's love for her creation.

Oak and Serviceberry's Message for Us

By superimposing structures of your unique design, humans create a connection with other aspects of Earth's life and processes. Language and history, discovery and analysis — these skills are a singular way of interpreting and comprehending the workings of Spirit. Humanity's role on Earth is ultimately to emulate.

Your primary strength is curiosity, which should be allowed to continue being the driving force of change. It would be helpful to open the channel even more widely, in order to have greater peripheral vision regarding incidental effects. Nothing moves in a vacuum — each thing tugs on everything else that is nearby.

Love manifests in humanity in a variety of tasks: parenting, teaching, giving spiritual guidance, producing foodstuffs, creating community, treating the sick, giving food and shelter to those who have less, coming together after great trouble to help and share, providing protection, and bringing inspiration into manifestation.

Recognize the good things in yourselves. Forgive, allow, see where there is lack and come forward to fill in the gaps. Anyone can make connection. However difficult it may sometimes be, see that good and evil are only different perspectives of the same circumstances.

We can show that Love is not capable of being destroyed — it will always be renewed and give of itself once more.

CHRONICLES

The Gambel oak is widespread in the foothills and lower elevations of the Rocky Mountains, and is slow-growing and of variable size. Under ideal conditions, it can reach heights of fifty to seventy feet, but is more often seen as a thicket-forming shrub. It usually disperses with the aid of animals like squirrels, woodrats and jays, which cache acorns in the ground. Gambel oak is drought-tolerant and well adapted to the extremes of the mountains. After a fire, it can re-establish itself from cloned root-sprouts.

Covering nearly ten million acres, its abundance makes it an important food source for a variety of animals—deer, elk, bighorn sheep, porcupine, rabbits and smaller rodents, who eat leaves and bark. Numerous birds, including wild turkey, grouse, magpies and woodpeckers, and small mammals, such as squirrels and chipmunks, favor the sweet acorns. The Colorado hairstreak butterfly lays its eggs on this oak, as the caterpillars find it a tasty food. It is also a prime roosting site for various species of bat. American Indians depended on the nuts of the Gambel oak, eating acorns raw, roasted, or ground into flour.

The western serviceberry, also called Juneberry, Saskatoon, or shadbush (so named because its flowers bloomed in early spring, "when the shad [fish] run") is one of about twenty species of related small trees and shrubs. Taken as a group they are native to all of Canada and the U.S. The fruit looks, tastes, and has a similar nutritional value to blueberries, and is another important food for wildlife—from songbirds and squirrels, to deer, elk and bears.

The serviceberry was essential to many Native peoples—not only are the sweet, juicy berries good fresh, but they dry like raisins and save well over winter. They have long been eaten by Canada's Aboriginal people as *pemmican*, a preparation of dried meat, like mincemeat, to which Saskatoon berries are added for flavor or as a preservative. Today they are used fresh in pies, jam, wine, cider and beer, and dried for use in muffins, cereals, trail mix and snack foods.

The Saskatoon serviceberry is listed as a Canadian heritage food by the *Ark of Taste*, an international catalog of foods that are in danger of extinction. This list includes native species, as well as traditional foods, plant or animal, "culturally or historically linked to a specific region, locality, ethnicity or traditional production practice."

The *Ark of Taste* is maintained by the international movement called Slow Food, which was begun in 1986 by Carlo Petrini, in response to the opening of a fast-food restaurant in a famous area of Rome, Italy. In protest against big international agro-business and the monoculture of fast food fare, it promotes the alternative: eating—and enjoying—local, traditional cuisine, prepared by local businesses, grown by local farmers.

< 159 >

The Slow Food organization, which sprang from this movement, has expanded to include more than 100,000 members in over 130 countries.

Slow Food has a number of related objectives: forming and sustaining seed banks; preserving heirloom varieties; developing regional centers that preserve local food products and recipes and celebrate local culinary traditions; organizing small-scale food processing, celebrations of local cuisine, and education of consumers about current food issues, amongst others.[26]

< The Rocky Mountains : Temperate Coniferous Forests : Gambel Oak/Western Serviceberry >

OAK/SERVICEBERRY COMPANIONS

Tiger Salamander
Wartberry Fairybell
Subalpine Buttercup
Wolverine

Colorado Hairstreak Butterfly
Western Monkshood
Green Lacewing
Hypomyces Lactifluorum Fungus
Columbia Spotted Frog

Limestone Columbine
Elk
Lark Bunting
Silverberry

Western Larch
Black and Red Stinkbug
Pussytoes
Townsend's Solitaire
Bearberry

Roots nosing through mineral cake,
tall ducting of trunk and branch, leaves
delaminating light
sent from a distant sun . . .

Lovest thou me?

The vein is struck, sap drawn,
the pits and fissures of the bark
are mined, buds
broken into, leaves laced.
There is also the toothtorn leaf.
the shredded shoot, the blindly hosted
fungal thread; the mealy kernel
of the nut bored,
its smooth case cracked . . .

Truly thou know'st

Flies glinting blue and gold
pulse on ripened fruit,
which spill their seeded juice
in beak and mouth, are pulled, pawed,
gathered by clever hands
or just drop from their own fermenting weight
to join other fallings
and passings, and crumblings
to dark mold and the wide earth
all of a lush litter . . .

Feed my sheep

FACTS ABOUT SOME OAK/SERVICEBERRY COMPANIONS

Elk

During breeding season, you can hear the sounds of male elk competing for domination of herds of females. The clash of antlers and loud bellowing can be heard echoing off the surrounding hills and mountains during late summer. Females are attracted to the males that bugle more often and have the loudest call.

There were once more than ten million elk across nearly all of North America, but now they live primarily in the West, especially in mountainous landscapes such as Wyoming's National Elk Refuge and Yellowstone National Park.

Early European explorers in North America, familiar with the much smaller red deer of Europe, thought the animal looked like a moose—the common European name for moose is "elk," and the name stuck. Elk are also called *Wapiti*, an American Indian word that means "light-colored deer."

Only the bulls have antlers, which start growing in the spring, and can help them reach a height of up to nine feet. A set of antlers, which shed and grow anew each year, can weigh as much as forty pounds.

Testosterone is the primary force in the formation and retention of antlers. After the breeding season ends, the level of pheromones diminishes and the testosterone levels of the males drop as a consequence. This drop in testosterone levels leads to the shedding of antlers, usually in early winter. Veins in the "velvet" on the antlers cools the blood before it is returned to the heart, keeping the elk cool in the summer.

They possess two canine teeth that are called "ivories," which are believed to be remnants of saber-like tusks that were used in combat by their ancestors.

Elk, like many species of deer, migrate to higher elevations in the spring and lower ones in the fall. The Greater Yellowstone Ecosystem elk herd numbers over 200,000 individuals, and during the spring and fall, they take part in the longest elk migration in the continental U.S. Elk in the southern regions of Yellowstone National Park and in the surrounding National Forests migrate south towards the town of Jackson, Wyoming where they winter for up to six months on the National Elk Refuge. Conservationists there ensure the herd is well fed during the harsh winters.

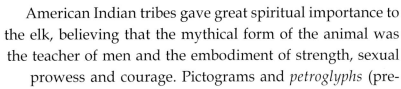

American Indian tribes gave great spiritual importance to the elk, believing that the mythical form of the animal was the teacher of men and the embodiment of strength, sexual prowess and courage. Pictograms and *petroglyphs* (prehistoric rock carvings) of elk were carved into cliffs thousands of years ago by the Anasazi.[27]

Larch

Larches are members of the Pine family, and although they are conifers, they lose their needles in the fall. There are several different species native to cooler parts of the northern hemisphere. The western larch, of North America, occurs in Canada and the northern reaches of the United States, where it is able to survive temperatures of nearly -60°F.

Larches are often used in bonsai culture, where their knobby bark, small needles, fresh spring foliage and bright autumn color are admired.

The Scottish sport of "Tossing the Caber" typically uses a larch tree about 19'6" long and weighing about 175 pounds.[28]

< 163 >

Wolverine

The wolverine is the largest member of the weasel family, and spends its time in the remote boreal forests of the north — the *taiga*.

Taiga is a Russian word, and describes the worlds largest land *biome*, found throughout the high latitudes of the northern hemisphere, between the tundra and the temperate forest. It makes up 29 percent of the world's forested land, where the dominant plants are coniferous trees.

A biome is defined as a "large ecological region characterized by similar vegetation and climate and all living organisms in it," such as: deserts, grasslands, tundra, forests, marine and fresh water.

An adult wolverine can weigh from fifty to seventy pounds, and is exceptionally powerful for its size. It has large feet, sharp claws, special teeth adapted to tearing off meat that

< The Rocky Mountains : Temperate Coniferous Forests : Gambel Oak/Western Serviceberry >

has been frozen solid, and oily fur that is water-repellent and resistant to frost. A carnivore, it hunts mostly hare and other rodents, but it won't go without food for days on end, like the wolf, and will eat carrion, dig into burrows and eat hibernating animals, or, on occasion, attack much larger animals than itself, such as elk and caribou.

The wolverine is not monogamous, but does form lifetime relationships with a small harem of two or three females, visiting them occasionally. Fathers stay in contact with their offspring until the kits are about ten weeks old. After they are weaned, some kits stay with their mother for up to two years, until they, too, are ready to breed, and some others reconnect with their fathers and travel with them for a time.[29]

Pussytoes

A member of the Sunflower family, this hardy wildflower grows in the foothills of North American mountain ranges. Emerging from a base of pale green leaves, it spreads by runners, and usually forms a series of connected mats that can cover an acre or more, if left undisturbed.

Colorado Hairstreak

The Colorado hairstreak butterfly was adopted as Colorado's official state insect on April 17, 1996. It may be found on both sides of the Continental Divide at elevations of 6,500 to 7,500 feet, in its usual habitat of scrub oak ecosystems. It depends primarily on the Gambel oak, for both food and habitat, and is found in the Four Corners area of the Colorado Plateau.[30]

Lobster Mushroom

The *Hypomyces lactifluorum* fungus is a parasite of *other* mushrooms, taking them over and transforming them into lobster mushrooms. They are named this because of the red-orange outer surface that covers the white inside. They apparently even have the taste of shellfish.[31]

Tiger Salamander

The most wide-ranging species of salamander in North America, it is the largest
land-dwelling salamander on Earth. The
tiger salamander is usually six to eight inches long, and lives up to fifteen years. Mainly
carnivorous, they will consume worms, insects
and spiders, small frogs and mice.

Tiger salamanders are primarily terrestrial, one
of the few species of salamanders able to survive in
the arid climate of the interior regions of North America. They
spend their lives in two-foot deep burrows below ground, near ponds, lakes, or slow-moving
streams, and are rarely seen in the open. However, they are born in water, and return there
to mate, often traveling long distances to return to their birthplace.

Their larvae are aquatic and, depending on the region, take a varied amount of time to
metamorphose. Some may not do so until they have reached adult size. These large larvae are
called waterdogs, and may be twice the size of the average adult, sometimes reaching sixteen
inches in length. Where the terrestrial conditions are bad, they may never metamorphose at
all, becoming sexually mature in larval form.[32]

< 165 >

Limestone Columbine

This type of dwarf columbine is very rare, and is located only
in rocky, limestone slopes and crevices high in the mountains
from Southern Alberta through to northwestern Wyoming.
Its violet-blue flowers sit on short stalks, just barely above the
foliage.

It is a *calciphile*, or a plant that requires alkaline soil to thrive.
Devoted gardeners will know that adding lime to their soil will bring
an acidic soil's pH level up, and may also know that the source of limestone is usually plants and animals that have died, their skeletons forming
deposits on the bed of a shallow body of water.

During most of the mid and late-Cretaceous Period, the water of the
Western Interior Seaway split the continent of North America into two halves. From approximately one hundred million years ago to sixty-five million years ago, it stretched from the
Arctic Ocean through to the Gulf of Mexico. At its largest, it was 600 miles wide and over 2,000
miles long, and filled with abundant marine life, from protozoa to huge dinosaurs and giant
sharks. The remains of these animals formed calcium deposits, which in turn formed the sedimentary limestone that now rests high in the alpine air of the northern Rocky Mountains.[33]

< The Rocky Mountains : Temperate Coniferous Forests : Gambel Oak/Western Serviceberry >

THE SILVER MAPLE

In hindsight, I feel fortunate to have spent my childhood in the country. Our house, the residence on a small cattle-ranch, faced what was then the main highway. The big pines in the front yard, their tops long ago truncated by high winds, made the property recognizable for miles across the rolling hills of northwestern Missouri.

Like much of that area, the woodlands had long since been cleared for crops and pasture, as the black, fertile soil went deep. Most stands of trees were limited to border fence-lines, riverbanks, and private yards.

From my bedroom window, I could see a century-old silver maple, planted during the construction of the house. During the '50s, although I only have pictures by which to estimate, it was probably between sixty and seventy feet high, but to me, it had a presence that overshadowed that of any other tree on the property.

Contrasting leaves flashed dark/light in the warm spring breeze, and later, hundreds of winged, A-shaped seeds helicoptered through the air. In summer, the broad canopy was shade for family barbeques, home base for hide and seek, and an awning under which I watched clouds and dreams of the future drift past.

Fall brought a carpet of soft, yellow-brown leaves gathered into tempting mounds and, like a watchful sentinel, the big tree was there after the school bus deposited me at the end of the drive. In winter, snuggling next to the radiator to read one of the many *OZ* books, I could see it outside my window, defying cold winds and snow, its arms waving in the wind.

The huge interstate highways that now crisscross America were being constructed then — Interstate 29 slowly emerged several miles east of us, linking Omaha, and the nearby town of St. Joseph, to Kansas City. While the highways served to unite the nation's population and industry, making growth possible, ironically, they aided in distancing us from our rural past, and an intimate relationship with nature that has now become a rarity to children.

My family, following the trend, abandoned farm life in 1965, and moved into St. Joseph. Sunday afternoons were frequently devoted to visiting relatives in Kansas City, and for a brief moment during the long drive, I could see the tall pines in the distance. The experience of adulthood beckoned, so I never returned to visit the ranch or my old friend, the silver maple. Missouri is prime tornado country, and a few years after we left, the big tree succumbed to the vagaries of nature.

ACKNOWLEDGMENTS

Producing this book has been the second biggest endeavor of my life. The first has been that of trying to live with my eyes wide open to my own intentions and effects—*this*, however, is an ongoing project, in which I hope to be engaged for many years hence.

That being said, there are many whose help and encouragement were fundamental to the development of this project; and to them I owe many thanks:

To Dolores, for believing that Magic will find a way—not simply to survive, but to allow for and flow with the times, and that it will make use of the vessels who offer themselves, whatever their abilities.

To my dear friends Cynthia and Estelle, for an invariable ability to dip into the well of enthusiasm and encouragement—you're the best. Many thanks are due to Silvia, Jeremy and Bridget, for your assistance with food, lodging and many years of friendship. And to Tol, for always being available to listen, after all this time.

To Brian, I am greatly obliged to you for the inspired poetic contributions, as well as insightful and dispassionate critiques, which you have provided, on demand, through literally years of changes.

To Ryan Parker from the Santa Ana Botanical Gardens, thanks for your assistance in finding the Laurel and Mexican Elder (via their Latin appellations), and driving me to their locations in a golf cart.

Special recognition goes to those who gave technical aid as well. To my editor, Jennét, for your advice, the excitement you have shown about this project, and for asking great questions, in addition to all the help with those tricky semi-colons, dashes and commas. To Mary and Andrew Neighbour, for the beautiful work they have done with the layout and photography, and the patience they have shown in dealing with an *artiste*.

And finally, to my sister Pat, thanks for your continued support for all my artistic undertakings, and for doing all that proofreading when I know you would have rather watched football.

SOURCES CITED

The websites listed here are intended for use by anyone who may be interested in further information on a referenced subject. There is no guarantee that these websites, as listed, will still be functional at the time of reading. In some cases, the website will have been updated and the web address changed, in which case a site may be relocated through a subject search.

CHAPTER ONE–NORTHERN PACIFIC COAST

1. "Proving That Slime Is on Their Side, Santa Cruz Students Make the Slug Their Mascot." *People Weekly*, June 16, 1986: 85.

2. Quinion, Michael. *World Wide Words*. Dec. 14, 2002. http://www.worldwidewords.org/qa/qa-huc1.htm/ (accessed July 26, 2011).

3. Suzuki, David and Wayne Grady. *Tree: A Life Story*. Vancouver, B.C: Greystone Books, 2004.

4. Fried, Rona. "Continental Conducts First Test Flight With Algae-Based Biofuel." *SustainableBusiness.com News*. Jan. 8, 2009. http://www.sustainablebusiness.com/index.cfm/go/news.display/id/17437/ (accessed July 26, 2011).

5. Hogan, C. Michael. "Rough-skinned Newt." *GlobalTwitcher.com*. November 4, 2008. http://www.globaltwitcher.com/artspec_information.asp?thingid=43182/ (accessed July 26, 2011).

6. Coulombe, Nikki. *Dancing with Trees*. "Arbutus." 2008. http://www.majestyoftrees.com/archives/category/arbutus/ (accessed July 26, 2011).

7. Oregon State archives. "About the Willamette Falls legend." *Oregon Blue Book*. http://bluebook.state.or.us/kids/symbols/teach/willamette.htm/ (accessed July 26, 2011).

Hear many short recordings of the Western Meadowlark singing at: http://www.youtube.com/watch?v=eArwzrFmdng&feature=related (accessed July 26, 2011).

8. Mosher, Dave. "Sea Lions Surprise Scientists by Adopting Orphaned Pups." *Wired Science–News for Your Neurons*: Nov. 11, 2010.

http://www.wired.com/wiredscience/2010/11/sea-lion-adoption/

(accessed July 26, 2011).

9. Kelly, David, *Secrets of the Old Growth Forest*. Layton, UT: Gibbs Smith, 1988.

10. Harris, Larry D. *The Fragmented Forest: Island Biogeography Theory and the Preservation of Biotic Diversity*. Chicago: University of Chicago Press, 1984.

11. Time-Life Books. *Myth and Mankind: Mother Earth, Father Sky–Native American Myth*. London: Duncan Baird, 1997.

< 169 >

< Thoughts and Dreams of North America Trees >

12. Angelfire. *SpiritSong*. Rattling-gourd, John. "The Origin of the Indian Pipe Plant." 2002. http://www.angelfire.com/ny5/spiritsong/IndianPipePlant.html/ (accessed July 26, 2001).

13. Pearce, J.M.S. "The doctrine of signatures." *Journal of European Neurology*, #60 (2008): 51-52

CHAPTER TWO–SOUTHERN PACIFIC COAST

1. The Wild Classroom Untamed Science. *The Wild Classroom*. "Biomes of the World: Chaparral." 2005. http://www.thewildclassroom.com/biomes/chaparral.html/

(accessed July 26, 2011).

2. Benett, Lynne, Esther Cheong and Hylke Dijkstra. *Oracle Thinkquest: Biomes*. "Chaparral." 2003. http://library.thinkquest.org/C0113340/ (accessed July 26, 2011).

3. World Wildlife Fund. *World Wildlife*. "Wild World Ecoregion Profile: California Chaparral and Woodlands." 1997-2011. http://www.worldwildlife.org/wildworld/profiles/g200/g121.html/

(accessed July 26, 2011).

4. Wilson, Bert A. *Las Pilitas Nursery*. "Nature of California–Platanus Racemosa." http://www.laspilitas.com/nature-of-california/plants/platanus-racemosa/ (accessed July 26, 2011).

5. Rasmussen, Cecilia. "*A Sycamore Deeply Rooted in City's Past*," Los Angeles Times, September 8, 2002, Local section. http://articles.latimes.com/2002/sep/08/local/me-then8 (accessed July 26, 2011).

6. Williams, Dr. David R. *The "Moon Trees"* N.A.S.A. April 1, 2011. http://nssdc.gsfc.nasa.gov/planetary/lunar/moon_tree.html/ (accessed July 27, 2011).

Miles, Kathy. *Starry Skies.com*. "Moon Trees! Have You got one in Your Town?" 1995. http://starryskies.com/The_sky/events/lunar-2003/moon.trees.html/ (accessed July 27, 2011).

The IB Traveler. "NASA hunts for lost 'Moon Tree' travelers of Apollo 14." *International Business Times*, 2011, Travel section. http://www.ibtimes.com/articles/110869/20110210/nasa-hunts-for-lost-moon-tree-travelers-of-apollo-14-photos-apollo-14-nasa-usfs-u-s-forest-service-u.htm/ (accessed July 27, 2011).

7. Jurek, Ronald M and Carie Battistone. "Resource Management: California Condor." California Department of Fish and Game. Updated June 30, 2011. http://www.dfg.ca.gov/wildlife/nongame/t_e_spp/condor/ (accessed July 27, 2011).

Kiernan, Tom. *Wildlife Protection/Wildlife Facts*. "California Condor–(Gymnogyps californianus)." National Parks Conservation Association. 2011. http://www.npca.org/wildlife_protection/wildlife_facts/condor.html/ (accessed July 27, 2011).

McLaughlin, Ken, Kelly Sorenson, et al. "Condor Reintroduction Program–Ventana Wildlife Society." *Big Sur Chamber of Commerce*. 1999. http://www.bigsurcalifornia.org/condors.html/ (accessed July 27, 2011).

8. Barlow, Connie. *TorreyaGuardians.com*. "Torreya californica (California Nutmeg)." 2005. http://www.torreyaguardians.org/california.html/ (accessed July 27, 2011).

9. National Wildlife Federation. "Garden for Wildlife: Making Wildlife Habitat at Home." 1996-2011. http://www.nwf.org/Get-Outside/Outdoor-Activities/Garden-for-Wildlife/Create-a-Habitat.aspx/ (accessed July 27, 2011).

McVittie, Janet and S.R. Meadows. "Growing a Natural Habitat Garden at Your School." *University of Saskatchewan: Teacher Resources*. 2011. http://www.usask.ca/education/coursework/mcvittiej/resources/garden/habitat_start.htm/ (accessed July 27, 2011).

10. Miyoko Chu. *All About Birds*. Bowman, John et al. "White-throated Swift." The Cornell Lab of Ornithology. 2011. http://www.allaboutbirds.org/guide/White-throated_Swift/id/ (accessed July 27, 2011).

11. Leonard, David Bruce. *Medicine at Your Feet: Plants and Food*. "Trametes Versicolor." 2000-2007. http://www.medicineatyourfeet.com/trametesversicolor.html/ (accessed July 27, 2011).

Gerstner, Louis V., Jr. *Information About Herbs, Botanicals and Other Products*. Memorial Sloan-Kettering Cancer Center. 2011. http://www.mskcc.org/mskcc/html/69194.cfm/ (accessed July 27, 2011).

12. Ballard, Gary G. *Kumeyaay.Info*. "Kumeyaay Elderberry Flutes." June 1, 2004. http://www.kumeyaay.info/indian_artifacts.html?http%3A//www.kumeyaay.info/museums/artifacts/elderberry_flutes.html/ (accessed July 27, 2011).

13. Keller, Jack. "Elderberry Wine: Taming the Wild Elderberry," *Winemaker Magazine*, April/May 2009. http://www.winemakermag.com/stories/issue/article/issues/109-april-may-2009/841-elderberry-wine/ (accessed July 27, 2011).

Keller, Jack. *Winemaking Homepage*. 2000-2011. http://winemaking.jackkeller.net/ (accessed July 27, 2011).

14. Zakay-Rones, et al, "Inhibition of several strains of influenza virus in vitro and reduction of symptoms by an elderberry extract during an outbreak of influenza B Panama," *The Journal of Alternative and Complementary Medicine* I, 4:361-9

15. Stallsmith, Audrey. *Thyme Will Tell*. "Enchanted Elder." 1998-2011. http://www.thymewilltell.com/elder.html/ (accessed July 27, 2011).

16. Center for Sonoran Desert Studies. *Especially for Kids*. "Fact Sheet: California Leaf-nosed Bat." 2006-2011. http://www.desertmuseum.org/kids/bats/california_leaf_nosed_bat.php/ (accessed July 27, 2011).

17. Dahl, William. *Botany.org*. "Parasitic Plants: *Sarcodes sanguinea*–Snow Plant." Botanical Society of America. 1997-2011. http://www.botany.org/parasitic_plants/Sarcodes_sanguinea.php/ (accessed July 27, 2011).

Armstrong, Wayne P. *Wayne's Word: Noteworthy Plants*. "Fungus Flowers." 2004. http://waynesword.palomar.edu/pljune97.htm/ (accessed July 27, 2011).

18. Sinervo, Barry. *BarryLab: Lizardland*. "The rock-paper-scissors game and the evolution of alternative male strategies." 1996-2011. University of CA, Santa Cruz. http://bio.research.ucsc.edu/~barrylab/lizardland/male_lizards.overview.html/ (accessed July 27, 2011).

Stephens, Tim. *UC Santa Cruz Currents*. "Cooperation between unrelated male lizards adds a new wrinkle to evolutionary theory." June 23, 2003. http://www.ucsc.edu/currents/02-03/06-23/lizards.html/ (accessed June 27, 2011).

19. Cecarini, Mario. *Cactus e Dintorni*. "The families–crassulaceae." 2000-2010. http://www.cactusedintorni.com/en/Succulents/crassulaceae.html/ (accessed July 27, 2011).

20. Smither, Bob. *Gulf Coast Turtle & Tortoise Society*. "The Red-eared Turtle–*Trachemys* scripta elegans." 2002. http://www.gctts.org/RedEaredTurtle/index.html/ (accessed July 27, 2011).

21. University of California, Irvine. *Natural History of Orange County, California*. Bryant, Peter. "Butterflies of Orange County, California– California Dogface: *Zerene* eurydice." 2011. http://nathistoc.bio.uci.edu/lepidopt/pieridae/dogfacm.htm/ (accessed July 27, 2011).

22. Waite, Mitchell. *WhatBird?* Dick, Gary O. "Green-tailed Towhee." 2002-2011. http://identify.whatbird.com/obj/617/_/Green-tailed_Towhee.aspx/ (accessed July 27, 2011).

23. John, Finn J. D. *Offbeat Oregon History*. "When banks closed, town of North Bend minted its own money–out of myrtlewood." August 29, 2010. http://www.offbeatoregon.com/H1008e_north-bend-myrtlewood-money-still-legal-tender.html/ (accessed July 27, 2011).

24. Kovacevic, Michelle. *COSMOS: The Science of Everything*. "Hummingbird sings with its tail feathers." January 30, 2008. http://www.cosmosmagazine.com/news/1829/hummingbird-sings-with-its-tail-feathers/ (accessed July 27, 2011).

25. Nafis, Gary. *California Herps*. "*Pseudacris* regilla - Northern Pacific Treefrog." 2002-2011. http://www.californiaherps.com/frogs/pages/p.regilla.html/ (accessed July 27, 2011).

Cabrera, Kim A. *Beartracker*. "Pacific Treefrog." 1997-2011. http://www.bear-tracker.com/treefrog.html/ (accessed July 27, 2011).

26. Ijichi, Dominic. *Seal Conservation Society*. "Northern Elephant Seal." 2011. http://www.pinnipeds.org/seal-information/species-information-pages/the-phocid-seals/northern-elephant-seal/ (accessed July 27, 2011).

University of California, Santa Cruz. *Science Notes*. Evans, Robert. "Real Seals Wear Helmets." 1987-2011. http://sciencenotes.ucsc.edu/9701/text/features/sealtxt.html/ (accessed July 27, 2011).

27. eNom, Inc. *Ehow*. Lindell, John. "Diet for a Grey Squirrel." 1998-2011. http://www.ehow.com/about_6524959_diet-grey-squirrel.html/ (accessed July 27, 2011).

28. Ewan, Joseph. 1973. *William Lobb, Plant Hunter for Veitch and Messenger of the Big Tree*. University of California Publications in Botany 67: 1-36

29. Beckmann, Poul. *Living Jewels: the Natural Design of Beetles*. Illustrated. New York, NY, Prestel Publishing, 2001.

Resh, Vincent H. and Ring T. Cardé. *Encyclopedia of Insects*. Waltham, Massachusetts, Elsevier/Academic Press, 2009.

CHAPTER THREE–PACIFIC COAST & GREAT BASIN

1. Oregon State University. *Volcano World*. Information Services, Oregon State. February 9, 1999. http://volcano.oregonstate.edu/ (accessed August 4, 2011).

2. National Park Service. *Experience Your America–Great Basin*. U.S. Department of the Interior. www.nps.gov/grba/ (accessed August 4, 2011).

3. Department of Geoscience. *Mountain ranges of the western United States*. University of

Wisconsin Division of Information Technology. September 30, 1985. http://www.geology.wisc.edu/courses/g112/mtns_westernUS.html/ (accessed August 4, 2011).

4. U. S. Forest Service. *Plant Database: Calocedrus decurrens, U. S. Department of Agriculture.* http://www.fs.fed.us/database/feis/plants/tree/caldec/all.html/ (accessed August 4, 2011).

Northeastern Area State & Private Forestry. *Incense Cedar.* U.S.DA./Forest Service. http://www.na.fs.fed.us/pubs/silvics_manual/volume_1/libocedrus/decurrens.htm/ (accessed August 4, 2011).

Muir, John, *The Yosemite.* New York, NY: The Century Company, 1912.

5. Youngquist, Ken. *Survivaltek – Teaching the Ways and Means to Survive.* November 3, 2007. http://survivaltek.com/?p=1822/ (accessed August 4, 2011).

6. D'Aoust, Pivoines. *La Pivoinerie D'Aoust – A specialized peony nursery.* 2011. http://www.paeonia.com/html/peonies/history.htm/ (accessed August 4, 2011).

7. North American Wildlife. *Wildlife North America – your online guide to North American Animals – American Pika (Ochotona princeps).* 2011. http://www.wildlifenorthamerica.com/Mammal/American-Pika/Ochotona/princeps.html/ (accessed August 4, 2011).

Clark Science Center. *Mammalian Species–Ochotona princeps.* Smith College. August 18, 1987. http://www.science.smith.edu/departments/Biology/VHAYSSEN/msi/pdf/i0076-3519-352-01-0001.pdf/ (accessed August 4, 2011).

Sierra Forest Legacy. *Biodiversity of the Sierra Nevada–American Pika.* Wilderness Society, Sierra Club, et al. 2007. http://www.sierraforestlegacy.org/FC_SierraNevadaWildlifeRisk/AmericanPika.php/ (accessed August 4, 2011).

< 173 >

8. eHow. *How to Videos, Articles & More – Trusted Advice for the Curious Life.* November 16, 1998. http://www.ehow.com/facts_5459584_cobra-lily-plant-information.html#ixzz1Fw0lZF4e/ (accessed August 4, 2011).

Pietropaolo, James and Patricia, *Carnivorous Plants of the World*, Portland, Oregon: Timber Press, 1996.

9. Society of Antiquaries of London. *Archaeologia, or, Miscellaneous tracts relating to antiquity.* 1838: Volume 29: 45, The Society.

10. Thinkquest–Library. *Arctic Animals–Caribou.* Oracle Education Foundation. February 26, 1998. http://library.thinkquest.org/3500/caribou.html/ (accessed August 4, 2011).

National Geo Wild. *Caribou–Rangifer tarandus.* National Geographic. February 14, 2011. http://animals.nationalgeographic.com/animals/mammals/caribou/ (accessed August 4, 2011).

11. Zahid S, Udenigwe CC, et al. "New bioactive natural products from Coprinus micaceus," *Natural Product Research* 20 (14) 2006: 1283–9.

Kuo, Michael. *MUSHROOMEXPERT.COM–Coprinellus micaceus.* September 3, 2001. http://www.mushroomexpert.com/coprinellus_micaceus.html/ (accessed August 4, 2011).

Medicinal Mushrooms–Coprinellus micaceus. Kaizen Publishing, Inc. 2011. http://healing-mushrooms.net/archives/coprinellus-micaceus.html/ (accessed August 4, 2011).

12. Eric Grissell, *Bees, Wasps and Ants: The Indispensable Role of Hymenoptera in Gardens.* Portland, Oregon: Timber Press, 2010.

< Thoughts and Dreams of North America Trees >

13. University and Jepson Herbaria Portal to California Flora. *Jepson Flora Project: Rosaceae–Rose Family*. U.C. at Berkeley. April 24, 1985. http://ucjeps.berkeley.edu/cgi-bin/get_JM_treatment.pl?6677,6695,6701/ (accessed August 4, 2011).

eHow. *How to Videos, Articles & More – Trusted Advice for the Curious Life/ Evergreen flowering plants*. November 16, 1998. http://www.ehow.com/about_6546036_evergreen-floweringplants.html/ (accessed August 4, 2011).

14. *Healthy Benefits of: Yarrow*. 2011. http://www.healthybenefitsof.com/p/yarrow.html/ (accessed August 4, 2011).

15. Natural Medicinal Herbs. *Medicinal herbs: Yerba Mansa–Anemopsis californica*. September 27, 2007. http://www.naturalmedicinalherbs.net/herbs/a/anemopsis-californica=yerba-mansa.php/ (accessed August 5, 2011).

Tucker, S.C. "Initiation and Development of Inflorescence and Flower in Anemopsis californica (Saururaceae)." *American Journal of Botany*, 72 (1): 20-30. Louisiana State University, Baton Rouge, LA, 1985.

16. About, inc. Hosting Operations. *Gardening.About.com*. "Xeriscape Gardening–Planning for a Water Wise Garden." March 12, 1999. http://gardening.about.com/od/gardendesign/a/Xeriscaping.htm/ (accessed August 5, 2011).

17. High Country Gardens. *Beautiful Plants for the Waterwise Garden*. October 7, 1996. http://www.highcountrygardens.com/ (accessed August 5, 2011).

18. Noel, Antonia. *venTREEloquism*. "Sunday Species: Thistledown Velvet Ant (Dasymutilla gloriosa)." April 11, 2010. http://www.ventreeloquism.net/2010/10/sunday-speciesthistledown-velvet-ant.html/ (accessed August 5, 2011).

19. Dole, Claire Hagen. "Phlox: A Butterfly and Moth Magnet." *Butterfly Gardeners' Quarterly: A Newsletter for Gardeners and Butterfly Enthusiasts*. 2000.

eNature. *eNature: America's Wildlife Resource*. "Spotted Langloisia – Langloisia setosissima ssp. punctata." August 19, 1998. http://www.enature.com/fieldguides/detail.asp?curFamilyID=838&curGroupID=11&lgfromWhere=&curPageNum=11/ (accessed August 5, 2011).

20. Wuksachi Lodge Sequoia. *Visit Sequoia–GIANT REDWOOD TREES & SEQUOIAS*. February 14, 2007. http://www.visitsequoia.com/redwoods-and-sequoias.aspx/ (accessed August 5, 2011).

21. Edkins, Jo. *Interesting Numbers: Fibonacci numbers and Golden ratio*. The Edkins family. August, 1996. http://gwydir.demon.co.uk/jo/numbers/interest/golden.htm/ (accessed August 5, 2011).

22. Hartesveldt, Richard J., et al. *THE GIANT SEQUOIA OF THE SIERRA NEVADA*. San José University, California, U.S. Department of the Interior, National Park Service, Washington, D. C.

National Park Service. *Sequoia and Kings Canyon National Parks Information Page*. June 17, 2008. http://www.sequoia.national-park.com/info.htm/ (accessed August 5, 2011).

Anderson, Dan. *Yosemite Online*. "Library: A Guide to the Giant Sequoias of Yosemite National Park (1949) by James W. McFarland – Comparison of the Giant Sequoia with the Coast Redwood." Yosemite Association. February 5, 2003. http://www.yosemite.ca.us/library/sequoias_of_yosemite/coast_redwood.html/ (accessed August 5, 2011).

A site of some interest for teachers and students alike: CALVIN CREST OUTDOOR SCHOOL:

The Spanish explorers who first observed these mountains, called them the Sierra Nevada, the "snowy mountain range." John Muir characterized them as "The Range of Light." Calvin Crest's goal as an outdoor school is to provide valuable lessons from this "Range of Light." Academically, skills such as observation and classification, investigating, recording and interpreting data are emphasized. Courses cover a wide range of subjects, including giant sequoias, the Miwok Indians, wilderness survival skills, logging and forestry, nature observations, and pond studies. http://www.calvincrest.com/

23. Long, Gary. *Wildlife Notes*. State of New Mexico Department of Game and Fish. January 31, 2003. http://www.wildlife.state.nm.us/education/wildlife_notes/WildlifeNotes.htm/ (accessed August 5, 2011).

24. Alcock, John. "Hilltopping in the Nymphalid Butterfly *Chlosyne californica* (Lepidoptera)." *American Midland Naturalist*. The University of Notre Dame. Jan. 1985: Vol. 113, No. 1, pp. 69-75.

25. Beug, Michael. *E-Flora BC: An Electronic Atlas of the Plants of British Columbia*. Mica-cap (*Coprinellus micaceus*). University of British Columbia. October 5, 2000. http://www.geog.ubc.ca/biodiversity/eflora/fungi.html/ (accessed August 5, 2011).

26. Gregor-Smith, Ben. *About Falconry*. December 13, 2010. http://www.about-falconry.com/golden-eagle-bird.html/ (accessed August 5, 2011).

Kochert, M. N., K. Steenhof, C. L. Mcintyre and E. H. Craig. *The Birds of North America Online*. Cornell Lab of Ornithology. 2002. http://bna.birds.cornell.edu/bna/species/684/articles/introduction/ (access August 5, 2011).

27. The Santa Barbara Botanic Garden. *SBBG–E-Newsletter*. "DUDLEYAS: – A CALIFORNIA SPECIALTY." 2011. http://www.sbbg.org/index.cfm?fuseaction=enews.article&article_id=136/ (accessed August 5, 2011).

28. Sharp, Jay. *Desert Biomes*. "Mountain Lion/Cougar/Puma *(Felis) concolor*." DesertUSA. September 28, 1995. http://www.desertusa.com/may96/du_mlion.html/ (accessed August 5, 2011).

National Geo Wild. *Animals: Mountain Lion–Felis concolor*. National Geographic. February 14, 2011. http://animals.nationalgeographic.com/animals/mammals/mountain-lion/?source=A-to-Z/ (accessed August 5, 2011).

29. Brown, Charles W. *Life Sciences*. Santa Rosa Junior College. October 19, 1989. http://www.santarosa.edu/lifesciences2/ensatina2.htm/ (accessed August 5, 2011).

5. U.S. Environmental Protection Agency. *Biological Indicators of Watershed Health: Indicator Species*. March 26, 1990. http://www.epa.gov/bioiweb1/html/indicator.html/ (accessed August 5, 2011).

6. Perlman, Howard. *The Water Cycle: Transpiration*. U.S. Geological Society–Georgia Water Science Center. 2011. http://ga.water.usgs.gov/edu/watercycletranspiration.html/ (accessed August 5, 2011).

U.S. Army Environmental Cleanup. *Phytoremediation*. September 17, 2009. http://www.youtube.com/watch?v=OUYTK9B2RSw/ (accessed August 5, 2011).

7. Auntie Canuck. *Organic Ade: Suck It Up! (AKA Phytoremediation)*. September 29, 1994. http://ourgardengang.tripod.com/whsuckitup.htm/ (accessed August 5, 2011).

8. Russell, Sabin, "Lizards Slow Lyme Disease in West." *Melissa Kaplan Reptile & Environmental Education*. October 9, 1998. http://www.anapsid.org/lyme/sceloporus.html/ (accessed August 5, 2011).

Scalise, Kathleen."Lizard May Act As Lyme Disease Panacea." *Berkeleyan*. April 29, 1998. http://www.berkeley.edu/news/berkeleyan/1998/0429/lizard.html/ (accessed August 5, 2011).

9. Rook, Earl J.S. *The Natural History of the North Woods: Red Osier Dogwood*. 1996. http://www.rook.org/earl/bwca/nature/shrubs/cornusser.html/ (accessed August 5, 2011).

Dictionary of Botany. *Dictionary of Botany: Far-red Light*. 2001. http://botanydictionary.org/far-red-light.html/ (accessed August 5, 2011).

Koning, Ross. *Plant Physiology Information Website*. 2004 http://plantphys.info/plant_physiology/phytochrome.shtml/ (accessed August 5, 2011).

10. Blumstein, Dan. *Marmot Burrow*. UCLA. 1995. http://www.marmotburrow.ucla.edu/ (accessed August 5, 2011).

"Groundhog Day." *Stormfax Weather Almanac*. 1996. Punxsutawney Chamber of Commerce. http://www.stormfax.com/ghogday.htm/ (accessed August 5, 2011).

11. AmberK & Azrael Arynn K. *Candlemas: feast of flames*. Woodbury, Minnesota: Llewellyn, 2001.

12. Butterfly Encounters. *Monarch Butterflies Eat and Thrive on Milkweed*. 1997. http://www.butterflyencounters.com/milkweed/index.html/ (accessed August 5, 2011).

Desai, Dr. Umesh R. *Cardiac Glycosides*. VCU School of Pharmacy. 2000. http://www.people.vcu.edu/~urdesai/car.htm/ (accessed August 5, 2011).

13. Lefler, Leah. *Hubpages*. "How Animals Are Domesticated: Domesticated Foxes Demonstrate Genetic Changes." 2011. http://hubpages.com/hub/How-Animals-Are-Domesticated-Domesticated-Foxes-Demonstrate-Genetic-Changes/ (accessed August 5, 2011).

14. Wilde, Megan. Chihuahuan Desert Nature Center. "Buffalo Gourds." September 23, 2010. http://cdri.org/nature-notes/plants/buffalo-gourds/ (accessed August 5, 2011).

Texas Beyond History: Lower Pecos Ethnobotany. Texas State University. August 13, 2001. http://www.texasbeyondhistory.net/ethnobot/gallery.html/ (accessed August 5, 2011).

15. Brown, Matt. *Celebrating Wildflowers*. "Plant of the Week: Clustered Lady's Slipper." May 9, 2011. http://www.fs.fed.us/wildflowers/plant-of-the-week/cypripedium_fasciculatum.shtml/ (accessed August 5, 2011).

< 176 >

< Secret Voices from the Forest >

16. U.S. Forest Service. *High Elevation White Pines*. 2011. http://www.fs.fed.us/rm/highelevationwhitepines/index.htm/ (accessed August 5, 2011).

17. Lanner, Ronald M. *The Bristlecone Book: A Natural History of the World's Oldest Trees*. Missoula, Montana: Mountain Press Publishing, 2007.

Lanner, Ronald M. *Made for Each Other: A Symbiosis of Birds and Pines*. New York, NY: Oxford University Press, 2006.

18. Helfield, James M. and Robert J. Naiman. "Keystone Interactions: Salmon and Bear in Riparian Forests of Alaska." *Ecosystems*. March 2006: pp. 167-180.

19. National Geo Wild. *Animals: Grizzly Bear Ursus arctos horribilis*. 1996. http://animals.nationalgeographic.com/animals/mammals/grizzly-bear/ (accessed August 5, 2011).

20. Forests, Lands and Natural Resource Operations - Province of British Columbia. *Ministry Home Tree Book: Black Hawthorn*. Province of British Columbia. October 30, 2000. http://www.for.gov.bc.ca/hfd/library/documents/treebook/blackhawthorn.htm/ (accessed August 5, 2011).

21. National Park Service. *Yellowstone: Nature and Science*. "Wandering Garter Snake." June 11, 2009. http://www.nps.gov/yell/naturescience/wandering-garter-snake.htm/ (accessed August 5, 2011).

22. Greiser, Tim. *Ask Nature*. "Increasing fire resistance: Arizona fescue." The Biomimicry Institute. October 11, 2007. http://www.asknature.org/strategy/67e42e0dc38567d258a3415dffcbc4a3/ (accessed August 5, 2011).

23. Seattle Audubon Society. *Birdweb*. "Red-breasted Nuthatch." August 25, 2000. http://birdweb.org/birdweb/bird_details.aspx?id=333/ (accessed August 5, 2011).

24. Cavendish, Marshall. *Endangered Wildlife and Plants of the World*. Tarrytown, NY: Marshall Cavendish Corporation, 2001.

25. Holoweb, Inc. *Solutions & Support for the connected world*." Painted Turtle–*Chrysemys picta*." 2011. http://www.holoweb.com/cannon/painted.htm/ (accessed August 5, 2011).

26. Petrini, Carlo. *Slow Food International*. May 7, 1998. http://www.slowfood.com/ (accessed August 5, 2011).

27. Raup, Bob. *Rocky Mountain Elk Foundation*. "Elk Facts." December 28, 1995. http://www.rmef.org/AllAboutElk/ (accessed August 5, 2011).

National Geo Wild. *Animals: Elk–Cervus elaphus*. 1996. http://animals.nationalgeographic.com/animals/mammals/elk/ (accessed August 5, 2011).

28. Scher, Janette S. *Plant Database: SPECIES: Larix occidentalis*. U.S. Forest Service. 2002. http://www.fs.fed.us/database/feis/plants/tree/larocc/all.html/ (accessed August 5, 2011).

Spence, Charles W. *Qi Virtual Marketing Group*. "Scottish Heavy Athletic Events–Tossing the Caber." September 16, 2000. http://qivmg.com/scottish/athletic.htm/ (accessed August 5 2011).

29. National Geo Wild. *Animals: Wolverine–gulo gulo*. National Geographic. 1996. http://animals.nationalgeographic.com/animals/mammals/wolverine/ (accessed August 5, 2011).

Wilson, Owen. *Slate*. Rastogi, Nina Shen. "How Strong Is a Wolverine?" April 30, 2009. http://www.slate.com/id/2217347/ (accessed August 5, 2011).

Patel, Daksha D. *Buzzle.com*. "Wolverine Animal Facts." June 21, 1999. http://www.buzzle.com/articles/wolverine-animal-facts.html/ (accessed August 5, 2011).

30. Colorado Department of Personnel & Administration. *Colorado State Archives–Symbols & Emblems*. State of Colorado. June 2, 1993. http://www.colorado.gov/dpa/doit/archives/history/symbemb.htm/ (accessed August 5, 2011).

Naberhaus, Thomas. *Butterflies and Moths of North America*. Big Sky Institute, Montana State University. April 26, 2006. http://www.butterfliesandmoths.org/species/Hypaurotis-crysalus/ (accessed August 5, 2011).

31. Wood, Michael and Fred Stevens. *Mykoweb: The Fungi of California*. 2004. http://www.mykoweb.com/CAF/species/Hypomyces_lactifluorum.html/ (accessed August 5, 2011).

Volk, Tom. *The Virtual Foliage Home Page! Tom Volk's Fungi: fungus of the month*. University of Wisconsin Madison Department of Botany. 1995. http://botit.botany.wisc.edu/toms_fungi/aug2001.html/ (accessed August 5, 2011).

32. Patel, Daksha D. *Buzzle.com*. "Tiger Salamander Facts." June 21, 1999. http://www.buzzle.com/articles/tiger-salamander-facts.html/ (accessed August 5, 2011).

Bond, Amelia. *A-Z Animals*. November 2, 2008. http://a-z-animals.com/animals/tiger-salamander/ (accessed August 5, 2011).

National Geo Wild. *Animals: Tiger Salamander–Ambystoma tigrinum*. National Geographic. 1996. http://animals.nationalgeographic.com/animals/amphibians/tiger-salamander/ (accessed August 5, 2011).

33. U.S. Geological Society. *USGS Geology and Environmental Change Science Center*. "A Story of Sea Level Changes in the Western Interior Seaway." February 14, 2006. http://esp.cr.usgs.gov/research/fossils/ammonites.html/ (accessed August 5, 2011).

Schmidt, Ron. *Ancient Sea Levels, North America, Cretaceous*. Pegasus Research Consortium. January 17, 2007. http://www.thelivingmoon.com/41pegasus/02files/Global_Warming_002.html/ (accessed August 5, 2011).

Bradley, James. *Scribd: Western Interior Seaway*. March 18, 2010. http://www.scribd.com/doc/28585962/Western-Interior-Seaway/ (accessed August 5, 2011).

ABOUT THE AUTHOR

Laura Merrill makes her home off-grid on a high mesa outside Taos, New Mexico. Her companions are several cats and a variety of wildlife including, but not limited to, coyote, pronghorn antelope, elk, endless bunnies and jackrabbits, ravens, mountain bluebirds, rattlesnakes, and tarantulas. The cats stay in, and everything else stays out.

During her association with a small spiritual community, Laura was encouraged to develop her natural ability to receive mental impressions—not only from other people, but from plants and animals as well.

Over the subsequent forty years, she has refined this capacity into a process by which she can communicate with the trees. No attempt is made to convince anyone that a tree has a consciousness that *can* be contacted—you may believe it or not, as Ripley would say.

Please visit www.laurajmerrilltreetalker.com for additional information.

About the Poet

Brian Mitchell has composed featured poems for each tree and the opening haiku for the chapters, using information Laura gathered from her communication with them. He and Laura became friends in 1971 through their mutual association with the aforementioned community. After thirty-five years of separately following their own pursuits, the two reconnected via the Internet, and have remained in contact ever since.

Brian spent several years in the U.S., living and working in New Orleans, Chicago, and St. Louis, Missouri, where he earned his Master's Degree in Creative Writing from Washington University. He is now retired and owns a rural freehold in Wales, where he writes, renovates, and has planted his own personal forest of over a thousand trees.

Please visit www.brianmitchellworks.net for additional information.